"This really is a great book. It will renew the romance in your life."

—*Michelle Valentine*
Time Warner Television

"A valid and nifty guide to wonderful places...and a bunch of little things to make the trip especially romantic."

—*Naples Daily News*

"A near guarantee of a great trip!"

—*Independent Publisher*

"*The Best Romantic Escapes in Florida* includes tips for romantic surprises, a list of inexpensive romantic extravagances and ideas for romance."

—*Orlando Sentinel*

"Unique and informative, with humor sprinkled throughout."

—*Buffalo News*

"If you don't happen to own a great romantic escape, *The Best Romantic Escapes in Florida* is the next best thing."

—*Donald Trump*

(Continued on back page)

Other Books by Pamela Acheson

More of the Best Romantic Escapes in Florida
(with Richard B. Myers)

The Best of the British Virgin Islands

The Best of St. Thomas and St. John,
U.S. Virgin Islands

Other Books by Richard B. Myers

More of the Best Romantic Escapes in Florida
(with Pamela Acheson)

Visiting the Virgin Islands with the Kids

Tennis for Humans:
A Simple Blueprint for Winning

The Best of the Peter Island Morning Sun

THE BEST
ROMANTIC ESCAPES
IN
FLORIDA

Second Edition

A Lovers' Guide to Exceptionally Romantic Inns, Resorts, Restaurants, Activities, and Experiences

PAMELA ACHESON
RICHARD B. MYERS

TWO THOUSAND THREE ASSOCIATES
TTTA

Published by
TWO THOUSAND THREE ASSOCIATES
4180 Saxon Drive, New Smyrna Beach, Florida 32169
Voice: 1-800-598-5256 or 904-427-7876 Fax: 904-423-7523

Copyright © 2000 by Pamela Acheson and Richard B. Myers

Printed in the United States of America

Library of Congress Cataloging-in-Publication Data
Acheson, Pamela.
The best romantic escapes in Florida : a lovers' guide to exceptionally
romantic inns, resorts, restaurants, activities, and experiences / Pamela
Acheson, Richard B. Myers.--2nd ed.
    p. cm.
Includes index.
ISBN 1-892285-01-0 (alk. paper)
1. Florida--Guidebooks. 2. Couples--Travel--Florida--Guidebooks.
3.Resorts--Florida--Guidebooks. 4. Hotels--Florida--Guidebooks.
I. Myers, Richard B. (Richard Brooks), 1946- II. Title.
F309.3 .A54 1999b
917.5904'63--dc21   99-057979
                                                              CIP

Cover Photograph: Byron Janes; Delray Beach

ISBN 1-892285-01-0

First Printing February 2000

For lovers everywhere

ACKNOWLEDGEMENTS

Special thanks to Juli Maltagliati Friedman

DISCLAIMER

The authors have made every effort to ensure accuracy in this book. Neither the authors nor the publisher is responsible for anyone's traveling or vacation experiences.

INTRODUCTION

This book is for everyone who wants a romantic escape. It's for people who don't have any time and want to steal a quick weekend away. It's for people who want to spend a blissfully romantic ten days together. It's for people planning for a very special anniversary or simply celebrating a new day of being in love. It's for people who want some more romance in their lives.

The escapes in this book and the romantic suggestions are here to make your life easier. Romantic lodging choices are paired with romantic things you can do once you arrive. With this book, you and your partner can pick a destination and make a few phone calls and quickly be on your romantic way.

By the way, Florida is an incredibly romantic state. If you thought all the sunshine state had to offer were flashy theme parks, palm trees, and spring breakers, then you are in for a wonderful surprise.

The truth is, the two of us moved to Florida reluctantly, but we fell in love with it fast. In fact we were dazzled. Great romantic restaurants and lodging choices abound. And it's one long romantic show for the senses here—vibrant sunrises, glorious sunsets, fragrant night-blooming flowers, salty ocean breezes, warm sun, giant moons that pop out of the sea, the lulling sound of lapping waves, the possibility of 70 degrees and sunny any day all winter long.

When could be a better time to go than now? So go find your partner and make time for a romantic escape—silk sheets and a shower together, sunsets on the beach, champagne or chocolate or flowers, floating together in the Gulf, a candlelight dinner for two, a dance in a crowd or a walk under the stars—whatever your romantic ideas, you'll find them here.

—P.A. and R.B.M.

TABLE OF CONTENTS

SPECIAL FEATURES

FLORIDA

MORE THAN 30,000 LAKES
8,426 MILES OF TIDAL COAST

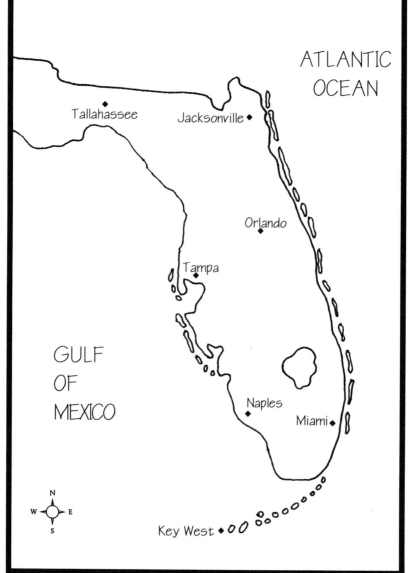

CHAPTER 1

ROMANTIC FLORIDA

FLORIDA'S ROMANTIC SCENERY

Florida's scenery is made for romance. There are miles and miles of exquisite sandy beaches, quiet waterways, peaceful lakes, splashy rainbows, and a profusion of brilliantly colorful and fragrant flowers.

Photographs and paintings of Florida sunrises and sunsets look gaudy and unbelievable but in real life these morning and evening sky-shows are spectacular. A thousand shades of orange. A thousand more of pink. Crayola crayons wouldn't stand a chance.

Flat land makes for a big sky and at night Florida's sky turns into a giant, dazzling canopy of stars. It gets dark here at night (the way it doesn't in big cities) and the odd result is that it doesn't really get dark. On a moonless night the stars are so bright you can see easily along the beach. Constellations present themselves in astonishing detail. Planets look too big to be real. The more you look, the more you see. Speeding satellites, twinkling planes, sensational shooting stars.

In Florida, you are always near water. It's only two to three hours from the east to west coast and you could easily watch the sun rise out of the Atlantic in the morning and watch it set in the Gulf in the evening. When you stay on the east coast, you can catch the sun and the moon pop out of the sea. On the west coast, you can see both slip beneath the water.

Over 50 kinds of palm trees grow in Florida but other trees grow here as well. On Amelia Island giant old oaks draped with Spanish moss shade the streets. Many west coast beaches are lined with tall and graceful Australian Pines.

Inland is romantic, too. The most northern part of Florida is similar to Georgia—forests of tall pines, red clay earth, hills. Central Florida farmland is flat, with green pastures and fields that stretch for miles, rimmed in the distance by thick groves of trees.

If you don't know central Florida, the first time you look at a map you will think there has been a mistake—it looks as if a soda can exploded and splattered the map with mini-size drops. The truth is, those are all lakes. There are over thirty thousand of them in Florida. These lakes are very calm and peaceful to look at. Gentle mist rises off them in the early morning. At night they reflect the stars and the moon.

Summer is the time of spectacular afternoon and evening thunderstorms. On the west coast they roll right in. On the east coast off-shore breezes have daily battles with the storms that barrel across the state. Some days it rains all the way to the beach and other days it pours two or three miles inland but never makes it to the shore. These rains can be torrential, but last only minutes, and the strong afternoon sun dries up the traces.

FLORIDA'S GEOGRAPHY

Beaches run the length of the barrier islands that lie along most of Florida's east and west coasts. These islands protect the mainland from the Atlantic Ocean to the east and the Gulf of Mexico to the west. Between these islands and mainland Florida is the Intracoastal Waterway. Bridges, locally called causeways, connect most of these barrier islands to the mainland. Many of these are drawbridges, which open (either at set times or on demand) for boats that are passing through.

Some of these islands are also connected to each other by bridges, but often you have to drive back to the mainland to get on to the next island. A1A is the name of the primary road that runs through all of these islands on the east coast. When you see a sign warning of the last exit to the mainland, that means, even if the road goes for 20 more miles, this is your last chance to get off the island.

In some spots the Intracoastal Waterway is quite narrow but in other places it winds through wide expanses of green and grassy marshes or acres of mangroves, and sometimes it is so broad that it is full of many little and mostly uninhabited islands. Two people can take peaceful canoe and kayak trips through these wetlands, and catch glimpses of rare birds, manatees, and dolphins.

FLORIDA'S WEATHER

In the summer, which runs from May through September, the weather is pretty much the same all over Florida—90s in the day, 80s at night. Breezes off the Gulf of Mexico and Atlantic Ocean keep the shores pleasantly cool and Florida's coasts are often considerably cooler in July and August than many northern cities.

Winter, however, is another matter. The temperature can vary by an important ten degrees. The average high/low in February in Jacksonville is 66/46 and in Palm Beach it's 76/56. Many places in northern Florida have fireplaces that you can retreat to on chilly nights. During a rare cold snap temperatures at night can drop to 28 degrees, even as far south as Palm Beach. On the other hand, on any given day, anywhere in Florida, all winter long, it can be in the 70s and sunny.

FLORIDA'S ROADS

Florida's road system is made for traveling. An Interstate runs north-south along both sides of the peninsula and travel is easy along either coast. Several major Interstates cross the peninsula. Back roads are plentiful and more scenic but they can take much longer.

A
ROMANTIC
MUSICAL MIX

Take along some of these CDs or tapes or your
own romantic favorites

Jimmy Buffett *Floridays*
Air Supply *Greatest Hits*
Dan Fogelberg *Innocent Age*
Any Sinatra
Any Elvis
Any Beatles
George Winston *Autumn*
Enya *Watermark*
Elton John *The One*
Carole King *Tapestry*
The Very Best of the Kingston Trio
Kenny G *Breathless*
Tony Bennett *Perfectly Frank*
Linda Ronstadt *What's New*
Liz Story *Unaccountable Effect*
Gordon Lightfoot *Sundown*
Aaron Neville *The Grand Tour*
Madonna *Something to Remember*
Survivor *Vital Signs* and *Greatest Hits*
Celine *All the Way: A Decade of Song*

CHAPTER 2

ROMANTIC CHOICES

THE CHOICES

Florida is filled with wonderfully romantic escapes. There's something for everyone here. However, one person's romantic dream can be another person's nightmare. Also, romantic moods change. One time the two of you might be looking for an elegant retreat where you can be pampered and dine at lots of fine restaurants. Another time you might want to hide out in a private suite at a small inn, or retreat to an out-of-the-way bed and breakfast where you can spend your days walking on the beach.

There are all kinds of romantic escapes in this book. Some are sophisticated and refined. Others are laid-back. Some focus on an incredibly romantic lodging. In other destinations, it's really the entire experience that makes it romantic.

It's almost impossible to feel romantic if you are stressed, so everything in this book is designed to be easy. Although several destinations are fairly remote, they are reachable easily on a major highway and close to an airport. Virtually all of the places in this book were chosen partly because once you get there, you can stay there. There's either enough to do on the property or many things you can walk to, if you feel like doing something. Romantic restaurants are within walking distance of the lodging or just a short drive so you don't have to get lost or mixed-up about directions.

HOW THIS BOOK IS ORGANIZED AND HOW TO USE IT

The book divides Florida into three sections: the East Coast, Inland Florida, and the West Coast. Destinations within the sections are in geographical order, not alphabetical order. This enables you to compare places that are near each other.

Each chapter starts with an overview of the destination. This is followed by a description of the most romantic lodging choice in the area, romantic places to dine, and suggestions of things to do.

Don't be startled if all the places in this book seem romantic. They are. That's the whole point of the book. The non-romantic places have been weeded out for you. You don't have to try to read between the lines to figure out if a certain place is actually romantic. All of these destinations are special and wonderful and romantic.

However, each destination is romantic in a different way. It's classier, or calmer, or cozier, or more remote. Sometimes it's the lodging itself that is incredibly romantic. Other times it is the experience of the whole destination. So choose what the two of you want.

Start by reading the overviews. Circle the words that appeal to you. Write "no" on the ones you don't like. Then look in more detail at the destinations that entice you. Then give the book to your partner and have your partner do the same thing (using a different color ink). Or go through the book together.

Or if you are already heading to a Florida destination (to visit parents or children, or for business reasons) this is the perfect time to attach that trip to a romantic escape. So look up destinations close to where you are headed . . . and sneak away together or meet there.

SECTION 1

FLORIDA'S ROMANTIC EAST COAST

**AMELIA ISLAND
JACKSONVILLE
PONTE VEDRA
ST. AUGUSTINE
DAYTONA BEACH
NEW SMYRNA BEACH
STUART
PALM BEACH
DELRAY BEACH
FORT LAUDERDALE**

◆ROMANTIC EAST
COAST DESTINATIONS

GEORGIA

ATLANTIC
OCEAN

◆Amelia Island

Jacksonville◆

◆Ponte Vedra

◆St. Augustine

◆ Daytona Beach

◆New Smyrna Beach

Stuart◆

◆Palm Beach

◆Delray Beach

◆Fort Lauderdale

GULF
OF
MEXICO

N
W ◆ E
S

CHAPTER 3

A ROMANTIC ESCAPE TO AMELIA ISLAND

AN OVERVIEW

This slender island is a remote and peaceful hideaway even though it's less than an hour north of Jacksonville. Majestic sand dunes, some as high as 30 feet, rim a stunning 13-mile-long beach.

The tiny town of Fernandina Beach is on the west side of the island on the Intracoastal Waterway. Here you'll find restaurants and shops and a remarkable 50-block area of Victorian houses built in the late 1800s when this was a prosperous shipping community. Streets are lined with towering old oaks draped with Spanish moss.

There are two exceptionally romantic properties here. If the two of you want to be right on the beach in a luxury resort that you never have to leave, choose the Ritz-Carlton Amelia Island. If you prefer to stay in an elegant bed and breakfast and walk to restaurants and shops and don't mind if the beach is a mile away, head for the restored, and very romantic, Fairbanks House in Fernandina Beach.

LODGING FOR LOVERS
RITZ-CARLTON AMELIA ISLAND

Come to this very elegant, self-contained, oceanfront resort for superb cuisine, gentle pampering, a spacious room, and nightly entertainment plus miles and miles of almost empty, wind-swept beach.

The beautiful drive here through grassy tidal marshes is a romantic prelude to the relaxation to come. Hold hands and take in the scenery. Once you arrive, you never have to leave, although the wide beach beckons for long morning walks and nighttime stargazing.

Rooms are hallmark Ritz-Carlton with classy, comfortable furniture and plenty of space. The two of you can stay in bed for days, ordering from room service and listening to the lulling sound of the ocean (which you can see from your bed). Or check in to the private-access Club Floor and relax in the living room and enjoy five complimentary food presentations daily (when one ends, another begins) and endless beverage service (including liquor, wines, and champagne).

Dine elegantly in The Grill, the resort's peerless restaurant, or the very casual Cafe 4750, which is open for all meals, and even has take-out. Do order breakfast in your room or out on your private terrace where you can enjoy the stunning view.

For the darkest and most intimate bar, step into the one at The Grill and listen to the soft music of the piano. The very large and very elegant Lobby Lounge has several rooms and many seating arrangements and it's easy to find a private place for the two of you to sit. Head here after dinner for a spin around the dance floor or find a dim and quiet corner and just listen to the nightly entertainment. There are miles of beach to explore and a state-of-the-art spa with a spacious indoor pool.

Billiards, golf course, tennis courts, indoor and outdoor pools, spa. Dress code: No tank tops, torn or faded jeans in public areas, no shorts in the evening. Jackets required in The Grill. Non-smoking rooms available. Check-out 12 noon. Romantic Packages. 449 rooms. 4750 Amelia Island Parkway, Amelia Island, 32034. Reservations: 800-241-3333. Tel: 904-277-1100. Fax: 904-261-9063. web site: www.ritzcarlton.com. $169-$269 plus $13/day valet pkg.

THE FAIRBANKS HOUSE

At this sophisticated bed & breakfast the rooms and suites are romantic retreats, many with their own fireplaces. It's not on the beach, but there is a lovely pool, and town and some of the best restaurants on the island are short walks away.

This restored 19th-century Italianate villa, which is individually listed in the National Register of Historic Places, is set way back from the road amidst exquisitely manicured lawns, brilliant flower beds, and tall old oaks draped with Spanish moss.

Each of the units is romantic and inviting. All are decorated with mixes of patterned wallpapers, deep hues of paint, oriental rugs, and antiques. All are romantic, but if you want to spend a lot of time in your room, the first and second floor suites are probably the best choice. Both are quite spacious, with a comfortable living room, a working fireplace (they'll supply the wood), a separate bedroom with a walk-in closet, and a bath with both stall shower and jacuzzi. The first floor suite has its own private entrance.

The heavy white terry cloth robes and turndown service with mints are nice touches. Ten rooms have fireplaces and six have jacuzzis. In back are two little cottages. You'll find coffee and tea on the dining room table from about 7:30 a.m. on. If the two of you want a full gourmet breakfast (served from 8:00-9:30 a.m), choose a table on the romantic little porch overlooking the gardens and service will begin (no advance notice needed). After breakfast you can stroll hand in hand through the gardens or relax in the comfortable living room with the newspapers or sit by the pool. The peaceful center of town is just a few blocks away and you can walk or bike to restaurants, shops, and boat rides. You can also bike a mile to the beach. At cocktail hour, guests gather for beverages and delicious hot and cold hors d'oeuvres. For a truly romantic treat, arrange for the carriage ride to a nearby restaurant.

Pool. No smoking inside or on grounds. No children under 12. Check-out 11:00 a.m. Romantic Packages. 8 rooms, 2 cottages. Innkeepers: Bill and Theresa Hamilton. 227 South Seventh St., Amelia Island, 32034. Reservations: 800-261-4838. Tel: 904-277-0500. Fax: 904-277-3103. Web: fairbanks.com. $125-$225.

21

RESTAURANTS FOR LOVERS

BEECH STREET GRILL

Tables here are on two floors of a charmingly restored house built in 1889. Although romantically dark, this spot can be somewhat noisy when crowded, so for an intimate dinner ask for a quiet table in a corner or by a window. A pianist plays upstairs Thursday through Saturday. Check the blackboard for excellent nightly specials. Crab cakes and house-cured salmon make fine appetizers. Local shrimp stuffed with crab, ginger and pepper-crusted roast pork loin, and seafood cioppono over linguini are excellent entree choices. The wine list is great. *Dinner only. 801 Beech St., 904-277-3662. $$-$$$.*

JOE'S 2ND STREET BISTRO

Despite the mundane name, romantics in the know make this a must-stop destination. Choose an umbrella table outdoors on the private, walled-in brick terrace or dine inside where deep green walls hung with art and blond wood furniture provide a peaceful background for an evening of romance. You might start with the Asian barbequed shrimp or the crab cakes or Joe's spicy gumbo. Fresh local seafood is a specialty here but the roast lamb, pork tenderloin, and grilled filet are also superb. End the evening with Champagne sabayon and a glass of port. Wine lovers will find the inspired list a true pleasure. *Dinner only. Closed Mon. 14 S. 2nd St., 904-321-2558. $$-$$$.*

LE CLOS

Step into this charming little yellow and white cottage for a delightfully romantic dining experience. Candles grace the tables in the two intimate rooms that are painted pale grey with white trim. Cuisine here is pure Provencale. Come for the escargot, the pate, the coquelles St. Jacques, the tender roast duck, and the steak au poivre. It can be a bit noisy here when absolutely full, but it's still definitely worth a visit. *Dinner only. Closed Sun. 20 S. 2nd St., 904-261-8100. $$-$$$.*

ROMANTIC THINGS TO DO HERE

Go on a beautiful drive. Drive south on A1A. Miles of road wind through grassy tidal marshes that are incredibly green in the summer and always serene.

Share a slab of chocolate peanut butter, chocolate walnut, or rocky road fudge at Fantastic Fudge *(218 Centre St., 904-277-4801)*.

Hop into Old Towne Carriage Company's *(904-277-1555)* horse-drawn carriages for a romantic ride for two in town or out to the beach.

Go on a sunset cruise for two. Sail Amelia *(Fernandina Marina at west end of Centre St., 904-261-9125)* offers -two hour sailing cruises.

Take a Biplane Ride over Amelia Island or over Cumberland Island with Island Aerial Tours *(1600 Airport Rd., 904-321-0904)*.

Explore the 50 blocks of astonishingly ornate Victorian houses. They were built by wealthy sea captains and merchants, who tried to outdo each other in conspicuous opulence.

Ride horses on the beach. Call Sea Horse Stables *(904-261-4878)*.

Stop by O'Kane's Irish Pub *(318 Centre Street, 904-261-1000)* for Irish coffee the way they make it in Ireland.

Watch the sun set over the marshes at Brett's Waterway Cafe *(Centre Street at the Marina, 904-261-2660)*.

Browse the appealing Book Loft for a novel to read together *(214 Centre St., 904-261-8991)* or a book on local history.

Enjoy looking through an array of authentic Irish goods—from handsome, handmade sweaters to walking sticks to sweet buiscuits—at Celtic Charm *(306 Centre St., 904-277-8009)*.

Take a canoe ride together. You'll find canoe and hiking trails at Big Talbot Island State Park just south of Amelia Island on A1A.

ROMANTIC RADIO
Light rock: 96.1FM   Jazz: 97.9FM
ROMANTIC REMINDERS
What to Bring: Jackets for the fancy Ritz-Carlton Grill, casual elsewhere.
Directions: I-95, exit 129. Go east on A1A 13 miles to Fernandina Beach.

23

A FEW OF THE MANY REASONS FOR LOVING FLORIDA

A BURGER ON THE BEACH

SAND IN YOUR SHOES

PELICANS DIVE~BOMBING FOR LUNCH

SHRIMP

MORE SHRIMP

FROZEN DRINKS

THE GIANT SKY

MANATEES AND DOLPHINS

FABULOUS BEACHES

SPECTACULAR CLOUDS AND DYNAMITE
LIGHTNING SHOWS

MANGROVES AND MARSHES

CHAPTER 4

A ROMANTIC ESCAPE TO JACKSONVILLE

AN OVERVIEW

The St. Johns River cuts a broad path right through the center of Jacksonville, a sprawling city with many distinct neighborhoods. High-rise buildings are clustered in the compact downtown area, but just ten minutes to the south is the splendidly peaceful residential section called Riverside. If it weren't for the cars offering a clue to the decade, you could easily think you had dropped back to an earlier era.

For serenity and solitude at a very romantic bed and breakfast, head to the beautifully-restored, Plantation–Manor Inn in Riverside. This is the place to come when the two of you feel like hiding away and just resting. There's nothing much to do here, except relax in your room, or perhaps sit on the porch, or go down to the beautiful pool, or make occasional forays out for a meal.

You can take a walk but there's really nowhere to walk to. The tiny (one block long) and charming village of Avondale, with several good restaurants, evening jazz, and one-of-a-kind shopping, is just a five-minute drive away.

LODGING FOR LOVERS
PLANTATION-MANOR INN

Built in 1905, this stately mansion is an exceptionally classy, quiet retreat. There's almost nothing to do. The two of you can talk, sleep, read, wander down to the pool, take a short drive to a restaurant for lunch or dinner. Rooms are beautifully decorated, well insulated from noise, and designed to be stayed in.

As you turn into the driveway, you feel as if you've driven into an incredibly peaceful sanctuary. Ahead are beautiful, well-spaced parking nooks, each for a single car. To the left is a stately mansion, surrounded by trees, with massive Greek Revival Doric columns supporting a second-floor wrap-around veranda.

The entire building, including magnificent cyprus woodwork, has been beautifully restored and thick insulation between rooms insures privacy. Indeed, even with televisions on, each room is a sanctuary. The nine rooms are lavishly decorated—mixes of wallpapers, fancy draperies, canopy beds, armoires, frilly linens.

All the rooms here are romantic in one way or another but they are very different from each other. One has a giant bathroom with a window seat for two, an old-fashioned tub that the two of you can soak in (cozily), and a modern shower. Another has a separate sitting area. Since each room is so different it's best to call to see what is available and then decide what you want. There's one room on the first floor. Five rooms are on the second floor and three are on the third floor.

On the first floor are several elegantly decorated (but very comfortable) living rooms and a dining room where a full breakfast is served at a large table. The mansion is set back from the road and there are lawns to walk on outside. A tall fence insures privacy at a long and pretty lap pool surrounded by a brick patio and shaded by leafy trees.

Pool, whirlpool. No smoking inside. No children under 12. Check-out 11:00 a.m. 9 rooms. Innkeepers: Kathy and Jerry Ray. 1630 Copeland St., Jacksonville, 32204. Tel: 904-384-4630. Fax: 904-387-0960. Web: www.plantation-manorinn.com. $140-$225.

26

A RESTAURANT FOR LOVERS
STERLING'S CAFE

Paintings adorn the deep-hued walls at this sophisticated spot where a flickering candle on each cloth-covered table hints at the romantic evening to come. The two of you can dine inside looking out to the avenue, but the most romantic seats are in the intimate room in back or the outdoor courtyard beyond. The menu is eclectic—try the fried green tomatoes or escargot or crisp calamari for appetizers; move on to grilled filet mignon or oriental duckling or the fresh catch, Japanese-seared or horseradish-crusted. It's quiet here even when it's crowded and this is an excellent choice for a romantic lunch or dinner. *3551 St. Johns Ave., 904-387-0700. $$-$$$.*

FOR AN EVENING OF JAZZ
PARTNER'S

Cozy up to the long bar or settle into a booth in this appealing brick-walled establishment and enjoy live jazz Tuesday through Saturday. The music starts at 8:00 p.m. during the week, 9:00 p.m. Fridays and Saturdays. *3585 St. Johns Ave., 904-387-3585.*

A ROMANTIC STROLL

For a look at what towns used to be like years ago, head three miles south to the tiny center of Avondale. It's just one tree-lined block long and amazingly quiet. There are only original shops and restaurants; none of the chains that have taken over so many main streets. Spend an hour just slowly browsing. **White's of Avondale** (*3563 St. John's Ave., 904-387-9288*) is a terrific independent bookstore where you can find great greeting cards, stationery, and gifts, plus plenty of books. Indulge yourselves at the **Peter Brooke Chocolatier** (*3554 St. John's Ave.,* 904-387-3827) with a box of chocolates or an ice cream cone while you stroll the avenue.

ROMANTIC RADIO
Soft rock: 96.1FM   Jazz: 97.9FM
ROMANTIC REMINDERS
What to Bring: Comfortable, do-nothing clothes.
Directions: I-95, exit 109 (Riverside). Right and go 8 blocks to Copeland St. and turn right.

Practical Packing for Lovers

Body paint – for the artist in all of us

Massage oils with sun screen

A small flashlight

A scented candle or two – to enhance dinner or bath

Something special and sexy for your partner to wear

Insect repellent and some sting-eze (just in case)

Lip "stuff" with spf - this is no time for chapped lips

Tapes, discs, videos if appropriate

Midnight snacks, some juice, other beverages

A couple of hats or bandannas

A surprise for your lover - that you both can enjoy

*A little stash of cash or travelers checks
for a special treat*

CHAPTER 5

A ROMANTIC ESCAPE TO PONTE VEDRA

AN OVERVIEW

Ponte Vedra Beach, which is right on the coast 20 miles southeast of Jacksonville, has been developed residentially as an upscale winter community and there are acres and acres of attractive and pricey houses but no real town of any sort.

Tucked amidst this development and right on the beach is the romantic Lodge & Club at Ponte Vedra Beach. This is the place to come when the two of you want to stay in one place and just chill out and do nothing but you also want to be able to walk right out to the beach, and you want the amenities that only a complete full-service resort can provide.

Here you two can settle into a room with a fireplace and a jacuzzi, step outside to the beach, walk across the street to a full-service spa, and wander into the comfortable lounge in the evening and listen to quiet music. However, if you feel like driving to shopping or restaurants, they're just five minutes away.

LODGING FOR LOVERS
THE LODGE & CLUB AT PONTE VEDRA BEACH

The spacious suites overlooking the ocean with jacuzzis and gas fireplaces plus the beachfront location and the luxurious spa are the romantic draw here.

With only 66 rooms, this full-service resort manages to have an intimate feel, although club members who live in the area can and do use the facilities. Rooms are in a tight cluster of four-story Mediterranean-style buildings with orange tile roofs. Don't be put off by the somewhat un-decorous cement walkways that lead to the units. Inside you'll find that the Ocean Suites are a comfortable, romantic haven. Although actually one big room, the cathedral ceiling, cozy window seat, and king-size bed set at an angle create a feeling of several rooms. There's also a kitchen area with microwave and small fridge and coffee maker.

A gas fireplace open on two sides lets you enjoy the fire from the bed as well as from the sofa. These are accomodations made for romance. Slip out of your clothes and into the thick cotton robes you'll find hanging in the closet. The spacious tile bathroom features a shower big enough for two as well as a separate two-person tub or jacuzzi.

Everything is easy for lovers here. There's 24-hour room service, a fancy restaurant, and a casual restaurant indoors and also by the pool. The bar and the lounge (with tea service in the afternoon, entertainment in the evening) face the ocean and even at night the scenery is beautiful because of soft lights tucked into the beachfront foliage. Thanksgiving and Christmas buffets here are outstanding—elegant and uncrowded.

There's close to a mile of beach and three pools, including one just for adults. There's a service charge of $12 a day plus 18% for restaurants and room service but no additional tipping is allowed. Not only do you come out about even, it's very relaxing to just sign your name.

3 pools, full spa, kayaks, bikes. Non-smoking units available. Check-out 12 noon. Many packages. 66 rooms and suites, 32 with gas fireplaces. 607 Ponte Vedra Blvd., Ponte Vedra Beach, 32082. Reservations: 800-243-4304. Tel: 904-273-9500. Fax: 904-273-0210. Web: www.pvresorts.com. $160-$385.

A RESTAURANT FOR LOVERS
TRA VINI RIST0RANTE
It's an easy drive to this elegant Italian restaurant and it's excellently-prepared cuisine and extensive menu. Tables are on two levels and there is a comfortable bar. Begin with the calamari stuffed with spinach or polenta with roasted peppers and provolone or share a shitake mushroom pizza. For entrees, it's a tough choice. Veal marsala, or a superbly grilled veal chop, or perhaps the shrimp and capellini. You can't go wrong. *216 Ponte Vedra Park Dr., 904-273-2442. $$-$$$.*

ROMANTIC THINGS TO DO HERE
Go horseback riding along the beach. Talk to anyone at the front desk and they will make arrangements with a nearby stable.

Bonfires on the beach are a specialty here. It may sound odd but they are wonderfully romantic. For a price you can have your own private bonfire for two along with after-dinner cordials and even a violinist.

Sail for a half- or full-day on a luxurious 65-foot motor yacht from Comanche Cove, which is about 15 minutes south at Vilano Beach.

Watch a movie and order up munchies—pizzas, popcorn, cheese board—from the room-service movie munchie menu.

Dine at the acclaimed Augustine Room at the Marriott at Sawgrass (*1000 TPC Blvd., 904-285-7777*). It's open for dinner only and reservations are necessary. It's about five minutes away by car.

Stop in and listen to the piano at Gio's Bar & Grill (*900 Sawgrass Village, 904-273-0101*) Tuesday through Saturday. This is a good choice for dinner, too. Try the filet mignon, rack of lamb, or osso buco.

ROMANTIC RADIO
Easy: 96.1FM   Jazz: 97.9FM   Oldies: 102.9FM
ROMANTIC REMINDERS
What to Bring: Bring your favorite CDs or buy one especially for the trip. *Directions: I-95, exit 103. East on 202 (Butler) to A1A. Go south 3 mi. to left on Corona. Turn right at Ponte Vedra Blvd. and drive south.*

WHAT IS ROMANTIC?

While researching this book literally thousands of couples from age 16 to 92 were asked: "What is the first thing that comes to mind when you hear the word romantic?" The most common responses were: candlelight dinners, the full moon, flowers, chocolate, diamonds, and champagne. But there were many other, more "individualized" responses. From the fairly common "sitting by a fire" to the far less common "pizza" and "crying," these are all actual answers.

flying kites
sitting by a fire
Sinatra
sharing pajamas
mirrors
weekends
ribs
waterbeds
pizza
skinny dipping
showering together
mud
poetry
thunderstorms
the past
phone booths
oysters
room service
nothing
sex
fun
vacations

hugs
naps
martinis
wrestling
limos
midnight
crying
sharing wine
hammocks
big bathtubs
whipped cream
violins
tan lines
sandy feet
matinees
no tan lines
sweat
elbows
Kenny G
smiling
Elvis
holding hands

CHAPTER 6

A ROMANTIC ESCAPE TO ST. AUGUSTINE

AN OVERVIEW

St. Augustine is located in northeast Florida, set on the mainland and facing the Intracoastal Waterway. Founded in 1565, it is the oldest continuously occupied European settlement in the continental United States. The compact downtown area of St. Augustine contains a remarkable collection of historical buildings, some dating from as early as the 1500s (Ponce de Leon discovered this area in 1513).

This a place for lovers to explore. There's one of the country's best preserved forts, the oldest wooden schoolhouse in the country, a number of fascinating museums, and a two-square-block, re-created Spanish village complete with "interpreters" re-enacting 18th-century life. St. Augustine is an extremely popular destination, and on weekends especially, streets and walkways can be crowded with visitors. Luckily, set right in the heart of the historic district, is the splendidly romantic Casa Monica Hotel. Built in 1888, and once owned by Florida magnate Henry Flagler, this castle-like escape is a perfect retreat for lovers.

LODGING FOR LOVERS
CASA MONICA HOTEL

Set in the heart of this historic city, this "castle," built well over a century ago, is a thoroughly modernized and appealing romantic retreat from the hustle and bustle outside.

The Casa Monica Hotel opened in 1888 and from then until the early 1930s it thrived as a fabulous winter retreat for wealthy northerners. Traveling south with trunks full of fancy gowns and dinner jackets, guests spent the chillier months living at the hotel and dining and dancing at charity balls and elegant parties. The depression put an end to the frivolity and the hotel remained closed until the mid-1960s when it reopened as the county courthouse. Then, in 1997 work began to transform the building back into the luxury escape that it is today.

The hotel is a grand structure covering nearly half a city block. The exterior has been fully restored to its original design. In the style of a Moorish Revival castle, it includes kneeling balconies, hand-painted Italian tile, arched windows, and five towers, the tallest reaching up seven stories. Luxurious two-story suites are tucked into the towers and showcase stunning views of the city.

The entrance is through an elegant lobby with marble floors, Moorish archways and columns, chandeliers from Syria, tropical ferns, and a fountain. Suites and rooms have been completely modernized and are decorated with Spanish-style furnishings: Picard-pattern draperies, wrought iron beds, wicker lounge chairs, mahogany tables. All rooms have coffee makers and safes.

On the second story, a large pool is set in a courtyard of tropical greenery. For a romantic dinner, dine at the 95 Cordova Restaurant. The dimly-lit piano lounge is a romantic spot to stop before and after dinner. There's also a casual restaurant open for all meals.

Pool, exercise room, gift shop. Non-smoking rooms available. Children welcome. Check out 11:00 a.m. Romantic Packages. 138 units. 95 Cordova St., St. Augustine, 32136. Reservations: 800-648-1888. Tel: 904-827-1888. Fax: 904-827-0426. Web: www.casamonica.com. $129-$519.

RESTAURANTS FOR LOVERS

95 CORDOVA

For a truly romantic evening slip into this enchanting Moroccan-decorated spot in the Casa Monica Hotel. The eclectic menu includes a delightful mix of culinary creations: Asian, Cajun, French, contemporary, and just plain southern. For appetizers try the French crepes wrapped around seafood, or the very fresh-shucked oysters, or the fried hominy grits with scallions and cheddar cheese; then move on to char-grilled mahi-mahi, yellowfin tuna on a bed of crawfish risotto, pork tenderloin topped with Creole sausage gravy, the catch of the day finished with a citrus-vodka glaze, or the unusual but superb duck pot pie. For dessert, double chocolate cake, warm apple pie, or the creme brulee are sweet choices. *115 Cordova St., 904-810-6810. $$-$$$*

ROMANTIC THINGS TO DO HERE

Check out the Castillo de San Marcos *(1 E. Castillo Dr., 904-829-6506)*, which took 25 years to build. It's a beautifully preserved, over 300-year-old fort, complete with drawbridge and dungeons.

Catch some blues and jazz at the Flamingo Room at Cortesses Bistro *(172 San Marco Ave. across from library park, 904-825-6775)*. There's entertainment Thursday through Sunday, starting at 7:30 p.m, at this bistro and espresso bar.

Create your own art gallery tour for the two of you. Look for the brochure "Art Galleries of St. Augustine" *(904-829-0065)*, which includes a map and description of 20 art galleries you can walk to in the downtown area.

Step way back in time and watch cobblers, blacksmiths, carpenters, and candle makers go about 18th-century daily life in the two-square-block Spanish Quarter Village *(29 St. George St., 904-825-6830)*.

ROMANTIC RADIO
Jazz: 97.9FM Easy: 96.1FM Classical: 88.5FM Country: 105.5FM
ROMANTIC REMINDERS
What to Bring: Walking shoes; comfortable, casual clothes.
Directions: I-95, exit 94. Go on 207 to US 1. Turn left. Turn right on King St.

DO NOT DISTURB
AND A FEW OTHER "DOS"

Do bring a "do-not-disturb" sign with you in case there's not one in the room. Of course you can call down for it, but you usually want it because you don't want to be disturbed.

Do bring your music with you. Sony makes a great little radio-CD player that's about five inches square and an inch thick. It's got great sound and even runs on batteries.

Do protect Florida's beaches. Don't walk on or play in the sand dunes or pick sea oats. It's a Florida law. What you wreck in a few minutes may never, ever come back.

Do unplug that little clock radio as soon as you check in so the two of you won't get wakened at 4 a.m. to the previous guest's choice of music.

Do marvel at how lucky it is that with over two billion people on the earth, you two managed to find each other.

Do go outside at night. As this side of the earth spins away from the sun, a sparkling nightscape appears. Look for shooting stars and satellites.

Do go down to the beach together just before dawn at least once. You probably won't see any other people and the light changes are stunning.

Do look at rainstorms in the distance. Sometimes you can be driving directly toward the storm—you can see the sheet of rain just ahead. And then the road turns and you aren't in it after all but you can see the rain just 20 feet away.

CHAPTER 7

A ROMANTIC ESCAPE TO DAYTONA BEACH

AN OVERVIEW

Daytona Beach is on the northeast coast of Florida. It is certainly a town more known for the Daytona 500, Bike Week, and Spring Break than for romance. And indeed, during motorcycle and automobile events, the town might be called exciting or even thrilling, but not traditionally "romantic." However, away from the special events, crowds, and cacophony, there is a relaxed, romantic side to the "world's most famous beach" that remains undiscovered by most.

Several blocks of downtown Beach Street have been steetscaped with wide brick sidewalks and now feature a variety of restaurants, coffee shops, and boutiques. By the way, Beach Street, despite its name, is not on the beach but instead runs along the mainland side of the Intracoastal Waterway.

Just a half mile further south on Beach Street, facing the Intracoastal Waterway and set under a canopy of live oak trees, is the charmingly restored Live Oak Inn and its own romantic restaurant, Rosario's.

LODGING FOR LOVERS
LIVE OAK INN

This historic 14-room inn is a charming spot for a romantic escape. It's across from the city marina and looks out to boats and the Intracoastal Waterway. There's an excellent restaurant right downstairs.

The inn is actually in two restored frame houses that sit side-by-side surrounded by shade trees in a quiet residential neighborhood across from the city marina. Both buildings are listed in the National Register of Historic Places. One was built in 1871 and is the oldest existing building in Volusia County. The other, built in 1881, is the oldest existing house in Daytona Beach. The site of the inn is said to be the site where Mathias Day founded Daytona.

These are truly old houses and stairs creak and floors squeak. Rooms vary in size but many are large and decorated with a mix of period antiques and more contemporary furnishings. Some of the rooms have jacuzzis and some have separate sitting areas and little private outdoor porches—a fine spot for a nightcap under the stars. Windows look out across the marina to the Intracoastal Waterway or to manicured gardens and trees.

If the two of you want to spend a lot of time inside your room, you might want to opt for the oversize Bill France Room with a claw tub in the bathroom and a jacuzzi in an alcove at the other end of the room. The very quiet and sizeable Day Room also has a jacuzzi.

In the morning come down and enjoy breakfast at a table for two in the sunny white breakfast room or out on the porch. There are several common living areas and complimentary wine and tea is served in the afternoon. The inn is set in a quiet residential area and there is no pool, and the beach is a five-minute drive away. All this helps make the Live Oak Inn a wonderful place to truly get away from it all.

Smoking outside only. No children under 13. Check out 11:00 a.m. Romantic Packages. 14 rooms. Innkeepers: Jesse and Del Glock. 444-448 S. Beach St., Daytona Beach, 32114. Reservations: 800-881-4667. Tel: 904-252-4667. Fax: 904-239-0068. $80-$150.

A RESTAURANT FOR LOVERS
ROSARIO'S
When the two of you feel like a romantic evening, just head downstairs to this intriguing Italian restaurant, which occupies the first floor of the Live Oak Inn. Tables are charmingly arranged in four different rooms. Italian-born chef/owner Rosario performs nightly magic in the kitchen while his wife Sunny deftly manages the dining room. You might begin by sharing the antipasto or having a bowl of homemade soup. Good dinner choices include the spaghetti putanesca, with sun-dried tomatoes, olives, capers, and anchovies; veal marsala; or scampi alla Rosario. Specials can include his popular, whiskey-infused Beef Manhattan. *Dinner only. Closed Sun., Mon. 448 S. Beach St., 904-258-6066. $$.*

ROMANTIC THINGS TO DO HERE
Look at all the gracious coquina stone homes along Palmetto Street. Just walk one block west.

Have a drink looking out at the Intracoastal Waterway at the Chart House bar *(645 S. Beach St., 904-255-9022)*, a pleasant walk away.

Take a cruise together. A Tiny Cruise Line *(401 S. Beach St., 904-226-2343)* offers a delightful excursion that leaves just across the street. When they say tiny, they mean tiny. This smooth, quiet 1890's style launch carries a maximum of 14 but they "always run, even with one," so you two might even have the boat to yourselves. Daytime cruises run year-round; the sunset cruise from April to October.

Take a backstage tour through the Angell and Phelps Candy Store and Chocolate Factory *(154 S. Beach St., 904-252-6531)*. The aroma is intensely chocolate (even the air must have calories here!).

Check out the architecture of the old Post Office on Beach Street.

ROMANTIC RADIO:
Jazz: 97.9FM   Easy: 1230AM   Classical: 88.5FM   Rock: 93.1FM
ROMANTIC REMINDERS
What to Bring: Casual clothes and yourselves are about all you'll need.
Directions: I-95, exit 87. East on US 92 to Beach St. Turn right (south).

CEREMONY & CELEBRATION

A wedding isn't just a wedding. It is a wedding ceremony. An anniversary isn't just an anniversary. It is an anniversary celebration. These are a couple of "big ones" but it only takes some minor adjustments to turn ordinary events into romantic ceremonies and celebrations. Try these at home or on your next romantic escape.

Light a candle, get out the good glasses, and turn a take-out pizza eaten on the couch into a romantic meal.

Pause and make a toast to your lover before you start a meal; it's a romantic ceremony you can even do at breakfast.

Pack a picnic and bring napkins and silverware instead of stopping at a fast food restaurant on a trip. Find a quiet park and share a picnic together.

Put on some music, share a glass of wine or an early dance, and then button her blouse, help him into his jacket, tie his tie. Getting dressed together for an evening out can be both a ceremony and a celebration.

Choose a special wine or a dessert to share and turn a meal together into a special celebration.

Celebrate all kinds of smaller anniversaries together: the day you found your first apartment; the night you knew you were in love; the day you decided to get married.

Dance together when a song that means something to both of you comes on the radio, whether it's in the kitchen or the shower or even walking down the street.

Hug each other and ask the question "How are we going to celebrate our love and the joy of being alive (and together) today?" when you wake up in the morning.

CHAPTER 8

A ROMANTIC ESCAPE TO NEW SMYRNA BEACH

AN OVERVIEW

Northeast of Orlando, on the northeast coast of Florida, is little New Smyrna Beach, which sits astride the Intracoastal Waterway. Its beachside half is unusually isolated and protected. In fact, it's the only town in the state of Florida to share a barrier island with a National Seashore and to have an unbridged inlet to both the north and south. Only the two bridges from mainland New Smyrna provide access to this unpretentious beach town. It's a unique situation that hopefully will be preserved.

It's the whole experience of being in New Smyrna Beach more than any one thing that makes a trip here romantic. There's a 20-mile-long beach, more than half of which is in the Canaveral National Seashore; the Atlantic Center for the Arts and its art gallery; plus casual restaurants and surf shops. The hard sand beach is wide and great for walking, although you must watch out for the cars that are allowed on parts of the beach during the day. At night the beach is almost always empty and a romantic place to watch for shooting stars. The charmingly restored Riverview Hotel is definitely the romantic place to stay.

LODGING FOR LOVERS
RIVERVIEW HOTEL

You can spend time in your comfortable room or out by the pool at this appealing and romantic inn. When you feel like a walk, the brick sidewalks of Flagler Avenue are right out the door, leading to restaurants, art galleries, shops, and the beach.

A brick walkway leads to this charming three-story inn, which is set back from the Intracoastal Waterway and just a short stroll from the Atlantic Ocean. The inn is surrounded by bright flowers and tropical shrubbery, and giant old oak trees create welcome shade. A wide veranda wraps around two sides of the building, and comfortable rocking chairs almost call out to have you come and set a spell.

A drawbridge crosses the Intracoastal Waterway here and the inn was originally built in 1885 as the bridge tender's home. There's still a drawbridge, although it's been modernized several times, and the home was thoroughly restored in 1984 and turned into a delightful inn.

The building has a Florida-style tin roof and is painted bright pink with white balconies and gingerbread trim. Comfortably decorated rooms vary in size and all but one have porches or balconies. Furniture is a mix of wicker and oak. The two third-floor honeymoon suites have four-poster beds and one has a nice view of the waterway. Breakfast is served in your room or on your balcony.

The common living room has been turned into an art gallery and just past the registration desk is a wonderfully imaginative gift shop. A tall fence covered with bougainvillea hides a large and lovely private pool. Just next door is the Ta Da Art Gallery and right beyond that, Heavenly Smoothies and Sandwiches, for tasty wraps. Along with its great location and inviting decor, Riverview Hotel's caring innkeepers are romantics at heart and have wonderful ideas for escapes for lovebirds.

Pool, bikes, gift shop. Children welcome. Check-out 12 noon. Romantic Packages. 19 rooms. Innkeepers: Jim and Christa Kelsey. 103 Flagler Ave., New Smyrna Beach, 32169. Reservations: 800-945-7416. Tel: 904-428-5858. Fax: 904-423-8927. Web: volusia.com/riverview/index.htm. $80-$150.

A RESTAURANT FOR LOVERS
RIVERVIEW CHARLIE'S

Right next door to the Riverview Hotel is Riverview Charlie's Seafood Grill, a romantic stop for dinner. Architect Will Miller has created a magnificent setting for food and drink at the water's edge. It's a stunningly designed space, with exposed brick walls, unexpected skylights, soaring ceilings, and big windows to capture the views. The menu offers seafood and steaks. *101 Flagler Ave., 904-428-1865. $$.*

ROMANTIC THINGS TO DO

See the current exhibit at Arts on Douglas *(123 Douglas St., 904-428-1133)* a stylish art gallery just across the bridge on the mainland. There's also a classy reception from 4:00 to 7:00 p.m. the first Saturday of every month, to celebrate the opening of a new exhibit.

Walk to Toni and Joe's *(309 Buenos Aires, 904-427-6850)* for lunch. Although you can drive, it's more fun to arrive from the beach in a bathing suit and bare feet. It's just past the lifeguard tower. It may look basic but the beers are ice-cold and the cheesesteaks the best anywhere.

Listen to Gino Conti sing love songs out on Riverview Charlie's deck from 7:00 p.m. until closing Wednesday through Saturday.

Pick up 18 or 36 icy cold, cooked shrimp with cocktail sauce from Ocean's Seafood *(601 E. Third Ave., 904-423-5511)* to take to the beach or back to your porch. This fresh seafood store also cooks several great daily specials to take out or eat in. Do sample the tasty dips.

Walk or bike along the beach for miles and miles. The swimming is easy (but be careful when the surf is up). Please don't play or walk in the fragile dune system or pick any sea oats. It's very harmful to the environment (and it's also against the law).

Get your hair cut together at Sandy Beach *(404 Flagler Ave., 904-427-6211)*. Ask for Sandy. She's great!

Stop by Beach Buns *(300 Flagler Ave., 904-428-7700)* for scrumptious baked goods, pastries, or tasty sandwiches. You can sit inside or out.

43

Drive down to the Canaveral National Seashore's beautiful beach. For details on trips and activities call the Park Ranger *(904-428-3384)*

Share a delicious pastry or pie or fabulous sandwich from Mon Delice *(730 Third Ave., 904-427-6555)*, an authentic French bakery.

For some casual and delicious Italian fare, stop by Vincenzo's *(410 Flagler Ave., 904-423-1895)*. Vince prepares each meal with care. His bride Annie adds dash and warmth to this friendly local favorite.

If deep sea or bottom fishing together strikes you as a romantic way to spend a day call Southwind Charters *(107 N. Riverside Dr., 904-423-9260)*. Captain John is the best around.

Pick up a bouquet for your room or have flowers sent as a surprise the day you get home. Just call or stop by the Pink Flamingo Florist *(806 Third Ave., 904-423-5927)*.

Stop by Victor's *(103 S. Pine St., 904-426-5000)* for a evening of inventive cuisine. The atmosphere is more festive than romantic (it's small, bright, and a bit noisy), so bring your own romantic souls and dine on grilled ostrich, blackened tuna, or BBQ chicken or ribs.

Look for a great gift at Ocean Village Treasures *(306 Flagler Ave., 904-428-3008)*. Stop by their Christmas annex.

Have dinner outside under the stars at Chase's on the Beach *(3401 S. Atlantic, 904-423-8787)* at the edge of the dunes two miles south of Flagler Avenue. See the fiery glow of the night shuttle launches here.

Browse through the colorful and creative selection of pottery at Palms Up Pottery *(413 Flagler Ave., 904-428-3726)*.

ROMANTIC RADIO
Easy: 107.7FM   '40s-'80s: 1230AM   Oldies: 105.9FM
ROMANTIC REMINDERS
What to Bring: Casual clothes, your surfboard.
Directions: I-95, exit 84. East on SR 44. Cross Intracoastal Waterway and left onto Peninsula Dr. Left onto Flagler Ave.

"DON'T BE SILLY!"

You have finally escaped together for some intimate and romantic experiences. You are away from the weight and stress of everyday life. This is obviously no time to be silly. You are adults. You should not do anything even remotely resembling the following. Certainly you wouldn't do them together. Don't be silly and...

walk in the rain

sing songs in the car

laugh out loud until you both cry

talk incessantly about why you love each other

stay up all night talking and hugging

go out for an ice cream cone, two scoops each

neck on the plane

kiss in the elevator

hold hands for your entire trip

fall asleep together under a tree

order eggs Benedict

have a Bloody Mary

take silly or risque photographs

send even sillier post cards to friends and family

lie together outside silently and just listen to life

eat a donut in the middle of the day

have a pillow fight

create a love poem for your lover

dance until your feet hurt

DECLARATIONS OF LOVE

Create an "official" gift certificate to be redeemed for a massage from you, or a shampoo, or a car wash — whatever your love would like.

Have a t-shirt or a hat or a bumper sticker made (check the Yellow Pages under silk screening/screen printing) that lets everyone and each other know you're in love: "Greatest Lover," "Love of My Life," "We may be old but we're still madly in love," etc.

Get a trophy made for your love. Award it for "Making My Life Wonderful" or "Best Spouse in the History of the World." It can be serious or silly.

Make a sign for the desk or the car or the boat shed that declares your love.

Hire a sky writer to draw your message of love across the afternoon sky.

Hire one of those aerial banner beach planes to fly up and down the beach saying "I love Suzy" or Fred or whoever your love is.

Write "I love you" on yellow post-it notes and secretly stick them all over the house—inside the medicine cabinet, in drawers, in closets, in the refrigerator; so your love will find them all day long.

Write "I love you" in shaving cream on the mirror.

CHAPTER 9

A ROMANTIC ESCAPE TO STUART

AN OVERVIEW

Stuart is a little town on mainland Florida, about 35 miles north of Palm Beach, on a peninsula of land that the St. Lucie River flows around to reach the inland waterway. The area is residential and grassy lawns run right to the water's edge. The river is broad here and very calm and good for canoeing or kayaking.

Tucked along the river's shore is a romantic bed and breakfast called the Harborfront Inn. It looks out across the water and there's a romantic swing built for two, a whirlpool with a view, and hammocks to laze in. The two of you can spend hours gazing out at the peaceful river scene, with clusters of anchored sailboats bobbing in the distance, and you can take a little boat right from the dock and explore the river, or even stay overnight on the sailboat that's berthed at the dock.

Amazingly, a tree-lined block away is a charming and romantic restaurant you can easily walk to. Just a one-minute drive away is a whole village of restaurants and shops and even a theater. Swimmers should note that there's no pool here and it's five miles to the ocean.

LODGING FOR LOVERS
HARBORFRONT INN

This tiny and peaceful bed and breakfast overlooks the river and you can sit in a whirlpool for two and take in the view or go in a little boat or a kayak right from the inn's dock. Restaurants are a short walk away.

Shade trees cover the soft mulch driveway and a manicured green lawn sweeps down to the water at this quiet stop. The original house was built in 1908 by a New England sea captain and combines deep blue trim and grey Nantucket-style shingles with the tin roofs so common in Florida. The architect who restored the original house and built two additional cottages obviously had a love affair with light and the outdoors. Windows in all sizes appear in surprising places, maintaining privacy but letting in lots of light and views of trees and sky.

Units vary tremendously here. You can choose one with a full kitchen or a separate sitting area or a jacuzzi. All rooms are deftly painted and wall-papered and in excellent condition. The furnishings and knick-knacks are an eclectic mix of old, odd, and antique, but together the result is comfortable and inviting. Dense insulation between rooms insures privacy from other guests. Some units have VCRs and CD players (and some romantic music CDs).

You both can explore the river together in the 12' Boston Whaler. Or charter the 33' sailboat for a trip to a secluded beach, or head out for an overnight sailing adventure. Spend evenings gazing at the stars or catching the full moon from the secluded outdoor whirlpool for two or have dinner served to you in the cozy gazebo.

There are many "weekend packages." Feel free to mix and match or design your own. The innkeepers are enthusiastically romantic and will arrange almost anything you have in mind.

Fees for 33' sailboat, 12' Boston Whaler, two-person ocean kayak. Smoking outside only. No children under 12. Check-out 11:00 a.m. Romantic Packages. 7 units. Innkeepers: JoAyne and John Elbert. 310 Atlanta Ave., Stuart, 34994. Reservations: 800-266-1127. Tel: 561-288-7289. Fax: 561-221-0474. Web: www.harborfrontinn.com. $85-$175.

A RESTAURANT FOR LOVERS

CASA BELLA

It's a short evening stroll to this Italian favorite. Every table is romantic at this cozy ristorante set in several rooms of a tiny old Florida house. Curtains are on the windows and classical music is in the air. Start with a Caesar salad or a soup (the minestrone and pasta fagioli are superb). Lasagna, fusilli with broccoli rabe, shrimp scampi, or veal picatta or marsala make excellent dinner choices. Additional tables are on a small, enclosed but breezy terrace. *512 W. 3rd St., 561-223-0077. $$.*

ROMANTIC THINGS TO DO HERE

Spend the evening at the award-winning Flagler Grill *(47 S.W. Flagler Ave., 561-221-9517)* for their prix fix once-a-month wine-tasting. Or come any night for an excellent grilled beef tenderloin, or herb-crusted snapper, or seared rare tuna—all outstandingly and creatively prepared. Stay for a fancy coffee and warm apple and cherry cobler or key lime pie or double chocolate brownie with ice cream. Go on your diet another time.

Start with the superb gorgonzola apple, and pumpkin seed salad and then move on to a grilled filet mignon or succulent crabcakes at elegant David's in the Courtyard *(Post Office Arcade Bldg.,561-219-4446).* Come early and have a drink in the comfortable bar.

Look for shooting stars from the dock. Listen for the soulful sounds of the train in the distance as you catch the sunset. The lapping water, the twinkling lights, and the stillness are very romantic.

Check out the Lyric Theater *(59 S.W. Flagler Ave., 561-286-7827).* Go to a play or a concert or an audience-participation murder mystery.

ROMANTIC RADIO

Easy: WGYL 93.7FM   Jazz:104.7FM

ROMANTIC REMINDERS

What to Bring: Your favorite CDs and video tapes, casual clothes, rubber-soled shoes if you intend to go boating.

Directions: I-95, exit 62. Go east 7 mi. to US 1 and turn left (north). Go to 2nd light (W. Ocean Blvd.) and turn left. Take 1st right onto Atlanta Ave.

AN INN, A BEACH RESORT, A BED & BREAKFAST
WHICH IS RIGHT FOR YOUR ROMANTIC ESCAPE?

RESORTS
Full-service resorts have hundreds of rooms and a complete array of services: 24-hour room service, a concierge, several restaurants and lounges, a spa and fitness center, a pool and a beach, and tennis courts and more.

Basically everything you could possibly want is right there on the property. Because they are larger and "everything" is right there, full-service resorts are busier than an inn or B&B. They are elegant and wonderful, but can be a bit less intimate once you leave your room.

INNS
Inns in this book have between 19 and 90 rooms. They were originally built to be inns. And with the exception of the Governor's Inn, all the inns in the book have a restaurant on the property. Many have room service available and will happily arrange for services that they themselves, do not provide.

Inns do not offer the range of services that one finds in larger resorts. Instead they offer a bit more charm and calm than their full-service sisters, a more intimate atmosphere when you leave your room.

BED & BREAKFASTS
Bed & Breakfasts range from as few as five rooms to about a dozen. They were originally built and used as private homes. Although there are restaurants nearby and some B&Bs can arrange for dinner to be served in your room, the B&Bs in this book do not have restaurants on the property.

Obviously you get a comfortable bed and a delicious breakfast but you also get much more. With a B&B, your experience will be more like staying at a friend's home. The innkeepers at the B&Bs in this book are as special as the properties. And they have a genuine interest in making your stay with them be as romantic and as special as it can be.

> **"There is nothing which has yet
> been contrived by man
> by which so much
> happiness is produced
> as by a good tavern or inn."**
> – *Samuel Johnson*

A FEW ROMANTIC EXTRAVAGANCES

Extravagance is sexy and romantic...and expensive. But you're in love so you might want to entertain a few of the following temptations.

Travel by limo. Have a limousine pick you up at the airport, or at your home, or take the two of you out for a night on the town. Dial 1-888-810-9111 for a limo at your door. It's a treat.

Rent a fancy car. Get a Corvette or a Jaguar or a convertible. If you're going to be driving, you might as well enjoy it.

Crash on the Club Level. If you've chosen a resort with a "club level" floor, go for it. It is more expensive but well worth it if you love food, beverages, and convenience.

Charter your own plane. Whether you want to land closer to your destination at a small local airport or actually at your destination (if it is Chalet Suzanne), a chartered flight can be a beautiful and romantic way to travel.

Swing for the suite. Whether it's the Honeymoon Suite or just an upgrade. What better time than now?

Go for the bubbles. Enjoy champagne or caviar or oysters or whatever is very special and celebratory for you both.

Splurge on flowers. Really splurge. If your love loves roses order a dozen for the porch, a dozen for the bedroom, a dozen for the living room. Don't forget a dozen for the bath, too.

Get tickets to completely sold-out concerts, plays, and sporting events. Call Global Tickets at 904-248-3232.

CHAPTER 10

A ROMANTIC ESCAPE TO PALM BEACH

AN OVERVIEW

Palm Beach, on Florida's southeast coast, is refined and flashy at the same time. Landscaping is gorgeous here and tall, perfectly-clipped hedges conceal palatial estates. On famous Worth Avenue, the quintessential draw for conspicuous consumers, luxury cars and limousines parade past pricey jewelry stores and designer boutiques.

Don't come to Palm Beach if you are searching for a beach. Come here to experience the superb service, to enjoy the cuisine in the elegant restaurants, to have a cocktail or two in the sophisticated lounges, and to dance together cheek-to-cheek.

The most romantic spot in Palm Beach is the blissfully romantic, very refined, and classically elegant Chesterfield Hotel, just off of Worth Avenue. Come here if you want an absolutely exquisite escape. However, if you definitely want beachfront, then check into the chic Four Seasons Resort, Palm Beach for a sophisticated and romantic getaway. Worth Avenue is just a ten-minute drive to the north.

LODGING FOR LOVERS
THE CHESTERFIELD HOTEL

When you're in the mood for a superbly elegant romantic escape, check into this jewel box just off Worth Avenue. From the exquisite service and decor to the sexy, X-rated Leopard Lounge ceiling, it's one of a kind.

The two of you will think you've somehow crossed the Atlantic when you check into The Chesterfield. Built in 1926, it underwent many transformations until 1989 when the owners of several classy London hotels purchased the property and imbued it with classic British style.

All units in this three-story hotel are stunningly and individually decorated (watch for the leopards, which turn up everywhere). Some rooms are small but the detail of the decor and the high ceilings turn them into cozy retreats. For a romantic splurge, the junior suites and full suites are outstanding. There's a spacious living area or separate room, plus a CD player and VCR. Some have two bathrooms. For a super splurge, request the lavishly decorated and very private fourth floor penthouse, reached by a private stairway.

When you feel like leaving your suite, the two of you can head to the large pool in the quiet courtyard or peruse the daily papers in the gracious wood-paneled library with a fireplace and comfortable leather furnishings. In the afternoon, enjoy High Tea—in the library, by the pool, or even in your room. For any service, just ask the concierge.

Dine elegantly at breakfast, lunch, or dinner in the intimate Leopard Restaurant. Have some wine and share a dance together in the Leopard Lounge; entertainment begins at 6:00 p.m. with a pianist and then a trio takes over. Take a good long look at the very sexy, X-rated ceiling. Room service is always available and elegantly served (try lunch in bed for a special treat). There's no need to venture outside the Chesterfield, but if you do, sophisticated shops and restaurants are just a block away.

Pool, library. Non-smoking rooms available. Check-out 12 noon. Romantic Packages. 55 units. General Manager: Alice Shaw. 363 Cocoanut Row, Palm Beach, 33480. Reservations: 800-243-7871. Tel: 561-659-5800. Fax: 561-659-6707. Web: www.redcarnationhotels.com. $99-$1099.

FOUR SEASONS RESORT, PALM BEACH

You never have to leave this seductive and ultra-chic beachfront resort. A highly-trained and responsive staff plus a full range of amenities make it incredibly easy to relax together. Just about anything the two of you want to do you can do. Just call down to the concierge.

Rooms are comfortable here and the most romantic ones have great ocean views but it's the service and the atmosphere that make the real difference. So check in and be pampered! Lie around the pool and be spritzed with Evian spray. Cuddle up in a private Honeymoon Cabana on the beach with a bell to ring for service. Be handed chilled iced towels to cool you off and warm linen towels to get the sand off. Head to the luxurious spa for a facial (yes, men get them, too) or dual massages (you can have these in your room also, at the same time). Stay in bed all day and have your room made up in the evening when you go down for dinner. Leave your shoes out at night and find them in the morning, magically shined and neatly tissue-wrapped with a gold seal.

The two of you can get dressed up and have a long and leisurely romantic dinner in The Restaurant, the resort's award-winning dining room. You can have a relaxed but intimate dinner in the dimly-lit Ocean Bistro, which is also nice for lunch indoors or out on the patio (or you can have lunch brought right to you while you lie by the pool).

Call room service and dine on your balcony or inside looking out at the view or watch a movie and order up cookies and milk or New York Style pretzels. The menus here are superbly creative—from the selection of snacks at the pool to the outstanding 24-hour room service choices—and the cuisine is excellently prepared. For the most romantic bar head to the dark and intimate bar in The Restaurant. There's also the larger Living Room bar in the lobby and another bar out by the pool.

Pool, tennis courts and pro shop. Dress code on season: no tank tops, faded jeans, cut-offs in restaurants and public areas; jackets required in The Restaurant. No-smoking floors. Check-out 12 noon. Romantic Packages. 210 rooms. 2800 South Ocean Blvd., Palm Beach, 33480. Reservations: 800-432-2335. Tel: 561-582-2800. Fax: 561-586-3393. Web: wwwfourseasons.com. $255-$2500.

A RESTAURANT FOR LOVERS
RENATO'S

Service is impeccable at this small and enchanting spot that is a short walk from The Chesterfield Hotel. Just inside the entrance is a tiny bar and a white piano, and a pianist plays softly as you dine in romantic elegance. Flowers are on each table, the atmosphere is hushed, and it is easy to forget that anyone else is around. So gaze into each other's eyes, share a bottle of excellent Italian wine, and enjoy classic Italian cuisine served on Limoges porcelain. For starters, the bresaola with goat cheese, the unusually light but excellent minestrone, or the roasted red peppers are good choices, but you really can't go wrong here. Pastas and entrees are superbly prepared. If you want something you don't see, just ask. You can also dine outside under the stars on their flagstone terrace. This is also a fine romantic place for lunch, too. *87 Via Mizner, 561-655-9752. $$-$$$.*

ROMANTIC THINGS TO DO HERE

Have a drink at the marvelous bar at Acquario *(upstairs at the Esplanade, at 150 Worth Ave., 561-655-9999)* where you come face to face with a stunning array of tropical fish. Stay for dinner at this award-winning restaurant and share a rack of lamb and flaming crepe suzettes. The menu is creative Italian, the ambience elegant.

Dance under the stars. At Chuck and Harold's *(207 Royal Poinciana Way, 561-659-1440)*, a portion of the roof actually folds back, opening the restaurant to the night sky. You lovebirds can dance under the stars!

Have brunch or lunch or enjoy late night entertainment at the legendary Ta-Boo *(221 Worth Avenue, 561-835-3500)*. There's piano until 10:00 p.m. nightly, a D.J. Friday and Saturday from 11:00 p.m.

Check out the sexy ceiling at the intimate Leopard Lounge *(363 Cocoanut Row, 561-659-5800)*. Come here early in the evening for a quiet drink and the sounds of piano, or later and dance to a trio.

Stop and have a drink in the Tapestry Bar (there's a pianist from 5:00 to 10:00 p.m.) and dine in the fabulous Florentine Dining Room of the famous Breakers Hotel *(1 S. County Road, 561-659-8427)*.

Dine leisurely together at the dimly-lit and romantic Leopard Restaurant *(363 Cocoanut Row, 561-659-5800)*. Reserve an intimate banquette along the wall and have a dance or two between each course.

Step back into the '50s and have an old-fashioned hamburger at Hamburger Heaven *(314 S. County Rd., 561-655-5277)*.

If you've slept late and want a fine lunch at 4:00 p.m. in the afternoon, slip into a banquette at Bice *(313-1/2 Worth Avenue, 561-835-1600)*. There's a great afternoon menu here and you are likely to have the place all to yourselves.

Dance after dinner Thursdays through Saturdays to the group at the Polo Lounge in the Colony Hotel *(just off Worth Avenue at 155 Hammon Ave., 561-655-5430)*.

Fantasy window shop along Worth Avenue. Most of the things you can buy on this avenue are stunning, but so are the prices. So create a romantic fashion fantasy for two. First perhaps some buttery-soft leather shoes for each of you at Ferragamo. Head to Van Cleef & Arpels for your diamonds. Trillion carries gorgeous men's and women's cashmere sweaters in a rainbow of colors. You might as well opt for them all. Of course, you'll need a new suitcase for all this stuff, so you'd better make your last stop Louis Vuitton. To re-enter reality, share a bottle of bubbly at Ta-Boo, and toast to the money you saved.

Get all dressed up. It's sophisticated here and it's romantic to be dressy. So pack your sexiest heels and your wildest ties and have fun primping and "getting ready"—together—for a romantic evening.

ROMANTIC RADIO
Jazz: 93.9FM   Classical: 92.1FM   Soft Rock: 104.3FM   Big Bands: WBDF1420AM
ROMANTIC REMINDERS
What to Bring: People dress up in season and jackets are the norm for dinner. Off-season, you can get away with more casual clothes, but why not have fun and get dressed up?
Directions: I-95, exit 52. East on Okeechobee Blvd. over Royal Park Bridge. Turn right onto Cocoanut Row.

COOL THINGS TO LOOK FOR

Millions of visitors come to Florida each year to see stuff yet they still miss some of the most amazing "stuff" you can see. Then again, maybe they aren't lucky enough to be in love and on a romantic escape.

THE GREEN FLASH. Catch it at sunset on the Gulf. You'll need a cloudless horizon to have a chance. Watch for a burst of emerald green just as the sun slips into the sea. There's no "maybe" about this one. When you see it, you really see it.

DOLPHINS PLAYING IN THE ATLANTIC. And the Gulf and even the Intracoastal Waterway. They are magnificent and you'll notice that they're usually traveling with a "significant other."

SHOOTING STARS AND SATELLITES. Whether you're on a beach or by a lake or in a park, Florida seems made for stargazing. Search for the constellations, wait for a shooting star, track down a satellite, or just hold hands and wish upon a star.

SPECIAL SHELLS. Look for Florida's special "gifts."

GRASSHOPPERS TO GECKOS. Great grasshoppers, little lizards, and a bevy of bugs are on parade all the time.

SUNRISES AND SUNSETS. They're ridiculously gaudy.

PELICANS FLYING IN FORMATION OR DIVING FOR DINNER. And sandpipers standing on one leg and looking silly, or the solitary beauty of a heron feeding as evening descends along the shore.

CHAPTER 11

A ROMANTIC ESCAPE TO DELRAY BEACH

AN OVERVIEW

Almost everything—boutiques, art galleries, restaurants, jazz clubs, an historic hotel—in this compact and sophisticated little town is on a one-mile stretch of tree-lined Atlantic Avenue that ends right at the beach. It's never really crowded, although it can be busy. Delray Beach, which lies between Palm Beach and Fort Lauderdale on the southeast coast, is much quieter, for example, than Fort Lauderdale.

Delray's romantic stop is the historic and seasonal Colony Hotel & Cabana Club. It was built in 1926 and, until 1997, open for only three months a year. It was a favorite wintering spot for northerners, who wouldn't dream of staying less than the entire season. In the spring the staff traveled north to Kennebunkport, Maine to run the sister hotel for the summer (also called the Colony). Now only some of the staff travel back and forth. The Colony Hotel & Cabana is open from November to early May. Come here if the two of you like the idea of staying in a quaint, rambling, old-fashioned, family-run hotel and want to easily walk to art galleries, restaurants, and outdoor cafes, and also right to the beach.

LODGING FOR LOVERS
THE COLONY HOTEL & CABANA CLUB

This romantic landmark has been run by the same family since 1930. The hotel is on Atlantic Avenue (the public beach is at the end of the street) but the Cabana Club (with pool and private beach) is a drive.

You feel the romance and the history the moment you enter this three-story, white stucco, Mediterranean-style hotel. The large lobby is filled with comfortable groupings of couches and you can imagine northerners gathered here years ago to while away the afternoon playing canasta. On the walls are photos of the owner's parents and grandparents and snapshots of the hotel in earlier days (it doesn't change, but the cars parked in front certainly do).

Rooms are small and, although simply furnished, feel more like a guest room in someone's house than in a hotel. The polished hardwood pine floors, soft blanket and soft white bedspread, the mahogany bureau with its own mirror, and the beveled mirror set in the closet door are all what you might find at home. Astonishingly, much of the furniture is actually the hotel's original furniture made by John Wannamaker in 1926. If you a want a little more space, ask for one of the several rooms that have a king-size bed and an over-sized bathroom.

The stairs are the quickest way to get to and from your room but for a bit of nostalgia take the ancient hand-operated elevator at least once. There's a tiny lobby bar and in the evening everyone takes their drinks out to the chairs on the veranda and later they gather here to listen to entertainment Tuesday through Saturday. On winter Mondays check out the cocktail party for the hotel guests. When the two of you are ready for the beach you can walk five minutes to the public beach or drive a mile and a half to the Cabana Club, where you'll find the hotel's heated pool and its own private beach and seasonal lunch restaurant.

Pool at Cabana Club. Smoke-free hotel. Hotel restaurant open for breakfast and dinner mid-Jan. to May only. Check-out 11:00 a.m. Romantic Packages. 66 units. Owner/General Manager: Jestena Boughton. 525 East Atlantic Ave., Delray Beach, 33447. Reservations: 800-552-2363. Tel: 561-276-4123. Fax: 561-276-0123. Web: www.thecolonyhotel.com\Florida. $69-$270.

RESTAURANTS FOR LOVERS

BENNARDO RISTORANTE

For a truly romantic dinner walk around the corner and up the street to Bennardo Ristorante, set in an old Florida house with a red tile roof. You'll see the red canopy entrance from afar and once inside you'll discover chef/owner Andrew Bennardo's dark and intimate retreat. There are just a few tables in each of the four small dining rooms. (On slow nights it's even possible to get a room just for the two of you.) There's also a cozy table by the fireplace. The menu includes several pasta dishes, a risotto of the day, veal chops, osso buco, and a very tender grilled duck that is served deboned and thinly sliced over a plate of roasted vegetables. *Dinner only. Closed Sun. 116 N.E. 6th Ave., 561-274-0051. $$.*

CAFE CIA TOTO

When you're both in the mood for some superb Italian cuisine day or night, just walk across the street to this inviting and intimate bistro. Choose a table on the sidewalk or a quieter one inside, where little square tables are draped in white under lazy ceiling fans. Listen carefully as the waiters describe the specials in thick Italian accents. Soup lovers will definitely want to start with the hearty pasta e fagioli. Good dinner choices include angel hair with a light tomato sauce, penne alle vodka, linguini with clams in a red or white sauce, veal chop in a gorgonzola-champagne sauce, and red snapper with white wine, tomatoes, capers, onions, and olives. This is also a wonderful place to come for a romantic lunch—try the shrimp Caesar or the lasagna with a glass of Pinot Grigio. *522 E. Atlantic Ave., 561-278-3837. $$.*

ROMANTIC THINGS TO DO HERE

For some outstanding live music in a sophisticated setting, step into the A-Train *(307 E. Atlantic Ave., 561-276-9092).* Wednesday through Saturday evenings, you can catch some great jazz, country fusion, soul, and blues performances. It's a different group and style each night so call for the current schedule.

Hold hands together and amble along the avenue. East Atlantic Avenue is a tree-lined street with wide brick sidewalks and 20 blocks of restaurants, bars, shops, boutiques, cafes, and art galleries.

61

Dine romantically at Vitorio's *(25 6th Ave. S., 561-278-5525).* "Food with a touch of love" is their motto. It's open for dinner only and closed on Tuesday. The decor is elegant and the cuisine is classic Italian.

Have lunch or dinner at the Blue Anchor (*804 E. Atlantic Ave., 561-272-7272).* This pub was actually the Blue Anchor Pub in England for 150 years (Winston Churchill used to stop by to have a pint when he was a Fleet Street journalist) before it was brought over here.

Go browsing in the art galleries. Find something you both like and take it home. And keep an eye out for some of the more outrageously wacky pieces. It's reassuring to find such humor.

Slip back half-a-century into Elwood's *(301 E. Atlantic Ave., 561-272-7427)* for a hot dog or a pulled pork BBQ sandwich in a setting filled with long-ago artifacts (like a 10-cent coke machine). There's music Wednesday through Saturday. Fridays, it's '50s classic rock.

Stop at Dakotah 624's Martini Bar *(270 E. Atlantic Ave., 561-274-6244)* when you feel like being where everyone else is. Stay for dinner.

Have lunch overlooking the waterway at Busch's Seafood Restaurant (*840 E. Atlantic Ave., 561-278-7600).* Return at night for the singer.

Drive to the Morikami Park and Museum (*400 Morikami Park Rd, 561-495-0233)* and wander through these quiet Japanese gardens.

Catch the live music at the Hoot, Toot & Whistle *(278 E. Atlantic Ave., 561-243-0140).* It could be Spanish guitar, or piano and vocals, or rock and roll. Call to see who's playing.

Check out the live entertainment at Erny's (*1010 E. Atlantic Ave., 561-276-9191).* There's something different almost every night.

ROMANTIC RADIO
Easy: LOVE93.9FM Swing/jazz: WDBF1420AM Country: 107.9FM
ROMANTIC REMINDERS
What to bring: Beach clothes, smart casual clothes for the evenings.
Directions: I-95, exit 42. East on Rt. 806, which is Atlantic Ave.

ROMANTIC SUGGESTIONS

Laugh. Be silly. Tickle each other. Tell jokes. Hide behind a curtain and scare your partner. Be kids together. Find the child inside you.

Be decadently lazy. Don't jog or run or play tennis or swim laps. Go back to bed after breakfast. Or stay there together until dusk.

Take pictures of the two of you. Bring a camera with a timer so you can take pictures of yourselves together: hugging, kissing, embracing, smiling.

Renew your vows on the beach at sunrise or sunset. This can often be done with very little advance notice. Check the yellow pages under weddings.

Dine at odd times. Eat breakfast at 11. Lunch at 3. Dinner at midnight. Restaurants are different places when no one else is around. You have the room almost to yourselves and the moments feel delightfully "stolen."

Avoid the "shoulds." Anytime either of you feels that you "should" do something, just don't do it. On the other hand, don't miss the stuff you'll wish you had done once you get back home.

Watch people rush back to work. If you are in a city, go to lunch late and linger. Savor the feeling of watching everyone else head back to work and enjoy your freedom.

SO YOU WANT TO BE AN INNKEEPER?

*Many people dream about completely changing their lives —
picking up, packing up, and opening a bed & breakfast.
Becoming innkeepers can sound so romantic.*

*A small number of people actually go for it each year. For
some it is a wonderfully romantic dream fulfilled, for others
a nightmare of monumental proportions.*

*If you have any serious thoughts about really exploring the
possibility of owning a B&B, you would do well to invest the
time and money and attend a "How to Acquire and Start Up
a Bed & Breakfast" seminar. These excellent classes are run by
David and Susan Caples, both experienced innkeepers, and
are offered six or seven times a year.*

*These weekends are enjoyable and extremely informative
and will help add reality to the romance associated with
owning a bed & breakfast. Seminars generally run Friday
afternoon to Sunday afternoon and include lodging, most
meals, and lots of input from professionals that will help you
really decide if you want to become innkeepers or just
continue dreaming about it.*

*For seminar dates, course descriptions, and prices, contact
LodgingResources.com Workshops, 98 S. Fletcher Ave.,
Amelia Island, FL 32034. Tel: 888-201-7603 or 904-277-
4851. Fax: 904-277-6500. Web: www.LodgingResources.com.*

CHAPTER 12

A ROMANTIC ESCAPE TO FORT LAUDERDALE

AN OVERVIEW

A huge number of restaurants, outdoor cafes, art galleries, and clothing boutiques are squeezed into a pulsating, six-block-long strip of Las Olas Boulevard, several miles inland from the beach. Sidewalks are crowded day and night and the atmosphere is frenetic and electric.

If there's a bit of the salsa beat in the romantic throb of your heart, then for a romantic escape you can't top the combination of Fort Lauderdale and the Riverside Hotel. The hotel is sexy (there are giant mirrors over some of the beds) and it's a peaceful hide-away, but when the two of you want to be where everyone else is, just step out the door.

If you like to be alone in a crowd, you can head to the outdoor cafes but you can also always find a dark romantic corner inside a restaurant if you prefer. To roam further, go out the hotel's rear entrance and catch a water taxi, which can travel the canals to a huge number of restaurants, museums, shopping areas, and even the beach.

LODGING FOR LOVERS
RIVERSIDE HOTEL

Lions flank the entrance of this charming, intimate, historic hotel which is right on trendy Las Olas Boulevard. Inside, cozy but romantic rooms, some with a giant ceiling mirror over the bed, offer quiet, sexy retreats from the "happening" atmosphere outside.

Two restaurants, room service, a newsstand, and a pool mean you never have to leave this small, full-service hotel, but when the two of you want to mingle with the crowds, find outdoor cafes, or look for late-night entertainment, all you have to do is walk out the front entrance onto Las Olas Boulevard. If you want to venture further, say to the beach, just catch a water taxi behind the hotel.

The most romantic units here are the Canopy-King rooms with the mirrored ceilings. They are quite small but rich dark fabrics make them cozy. The king-size bed takes up most of the room but it's where you may want to spend most of your time anyway, having fun with the mirrored ceiling. All units are tastefully decorated and some have balconies and views of Las Olas Boulevard or the waterway. Dark curtains keep the daylight out for long naps. Restaurants are open late, so you don't have to worry about missing a meal. The hotel was built in 1936 and bathrooms have been remodeled but are still small. All rooms have a little refrigerator.

Downstairs, the Golden Lyon Lounge is a quiet spot for a drink (except during the bustling happy hour). For lunch or dinner, Indigo serves Indonesian and Malaysian cuisine outdoors and in (the quietest, most romantic table is inside by the fireplace). The Grill Room is a romantic dinner spot. In the afternoon, the two of you can order Royal Tea, an extravaganza that includes port wine and champagne, in the gracious lobby with gas fireplaces and comfortable rattan couches.

Pool. Parking fee: $6 per day. Non-smoking rooms available. Children welcome. Check-out 11:00 a.m. Romantic Packages. 109 rooms and suites. 620 East Las Olas Blvd., Fort Lauderdale, 33301. Reservations: 800-325-3280. Tel: 954-467-0671. Fax: 954-462-2148. Web: www.riversidehotel.com. $119-$299.

RESTAURANTS FOR LOVERS

Many restaurants along Las Olas Boulevard have indoor and outdoor seating but the traffic noise can be jarring and generally the indoor seating is quieter and more conducive to romance.

GALLERIA G'VANNI

Giant oil paintings of James Dean, Marilyn Monroe, and others with a claim to fame hang on the walls of this casual Italian spot across the street from the Riverside Hotel. There are tables outside but it's darker, quieter, and more romantic inside (until around 10:00 p.m. that is, when the live entertainment rolls in). The pasta fagioli is superb and so is the wilted spinach with raisins and pine nuts. Entrees include a variety of classic pastas, veal, and chicken dishes. *625 E. Las Olas Blvd., 954-524-5246. $$.*

GRILL ROOM ON LAS OLAS

This dark and captivating restaurant combines couches and chairs for intimate seating arrangements. Settle in and be prepared for a world-class dining experience with excellent service. If you want, share everything: the Caesar salad prepared tableside, the chateaubriand carved tableside or the roast rack of lamb, and a bottle of red from the extensive wine list. The mostly Continental menu includes a wide selection of steaks (filet, strip, rib), plus roasted duck, sesame seared tuna, and pumpkin-crusted snapper. There's a martini menu, oysters and caviar on the appetizer menu, and a stunning wine room. There are outside tables also. *Dinner only. Riverside Hotel, 620 E. Las Olas Blvd., 954-467-0671. $$-$$$.*

LAS OLAS CAFE

This quiet, hidden-away spot just steps back from Las Olas Boulevard is indeed romantic, especially outdoors. Follow the walkway to the secluded courtyard and dine outside under the stars (there's also an intimate little indoor dining room). The cuisine is creative and superbly prepared. Try the shrimp stuffed with mozarella or the chicken quesadilla or the retro apple and walnut salad for a start and then move on to walnut-crusted fresh fish or blackened shrimp or pasta Andre— penne pasta with spinach, mushrooms, and fresh tomatoes. *922 E. Las Olas Blvd., 954-524-4300. $$.*

LE CAFE DE PARIS

At this quiet and very French restaurant, you can dine outdoors but inside it's more peaceful and intimate and delightfully dark. There are meals to share: Steak Diane and Filet au Poivre Flambe au Cognac are prepared at your table and there's a wonderful section of the menu devoted just to Celebration Dinners for Two. These include wine or champagne, a Caesar salad for two, a selection of entrees to be shared (the Beef Wellington and the Veal Cordon Bleu are excellent) and a scrumptious Baked Alaska for Two. Other house specialties are bouillabaisse, shrimp scampi, and roasted duck. *No lunch Sun. 715 E. Las Olas Blvd., 954-467-2900. $$-$$$.*

ROMANTIC THINGS TO DO HERE

Buy each other a CD or a book, then have a capuccino and listen to live music (it might be jazz or acoustic guitar) at the appealing Liberties *(888 E. Las Olas Blvd., 954-522-6789)*. It's much more than a bookstore.

Pick up a love potion, silky body creams, and aromatic oils at Goodebodies *(920 Las Olas Blvd., 954-462-2551)*.

Spend an evening enjoying fine French cuisine and the keyboard player at the French Quarter *(215 S.E. 8th Ave., 954-465-8000)* Wednesdays through Saturdays. This is a romantic lunch spot, too.

For the trendiest restaurant decor and cuisine, don't miss stunning Mark's Las Olas *(1032 E. Las Olas Blvd., 954-463-1000)*. At least stop by for a drink.

Hold hands and browse up and down the boulevard. Check out the shops and galleries, stopping for a snack or a drink at an outside cafe.

ROMANTIC RADIO

Easy: 93.9FM   Classical: 93.1FM   '70s-'80s: 97.3FM

ROMANTIC REMINDERS

What to Bring: Something sexy to wear under the ceiling mirrors.
Directions: I-95, exit 29 (Broward Blvd.). East to US 1. South on US 1 to Las Olas Blvd. and turn east (left). Turn right on 6th Ave. and then take your first left. You'll see the hotel on your left.

WATCH OUT!

Following are some of the less wonderful things Florida offers that you might want to "watch out" for, a few things that might reduce the romance of your escape.

JACK SPANIELS. No they're not dogs, they're colorful insects that look a bit like wasps. They also sting like wasps.

GOAT'S HEADS OR SAND SPURS. These little spiked balls can turn up anywhere, from the path through the dunes to the beach, to a grassy area of a park. It is a good idea to wear something on your feet. You'll avoid the pain and bouncing around on one foot trying to extract these stinkers.

SHIRTS AND SHOES. Speaking of shoes, Florida law requires that you wear shirts and shoes in restaurants, bars, and stores that sell food. If you're going to walk on a beach to "civilization" remember to bring at least flip-flops and a top.

FIRE ANTS. These little devils did not get their name by working for the local fire department. The safest way to avoid their fire-like sting is to avoid anything that looks like an ant when you are outside.

THUNDERSTORMS. They are romantic and magnificent to watch. Do this from inside. You are in the lightning capital of the country. And lightning is a killer.

THE DRIVERS. Florida has a volatile combination of retired people in no hurry to go anywhere, locals who are always in a hurry to get somewhere, and tourists who don't know where they're going anyway. Drive defensively so you'll be able to enjoy more romantic escapes in the future.

WHAT DO YOU WANT?

When you already have certain criteria for your romantic escape, you can use this chart to identify the properties that fit what you want.

RIGHT ON THE BEACH
Four Seasons Resort, Palm Beach
Harrington House
Lodge & Club at Ponte Vedra Beach
Palm Island Resort
Ritz-Carlton Amelia Island
Song of the Sea

ANTIQUES
Ft. Lauderdale
Mount Dora
Naples
Palm Beach
St. Augustine
Winter Park

RESTAURANTS AND BARS WITHIN AN EASY WALK
Casa Monica Hotel
Celebration Hotel
Chesterfield Hotel
Colony Hotel & Cabana Club
Fairbanks House
Lakeside Inn
Live Oak Inn
Park Plaza Hotel
Riverview Hotel
Riverside Hotel
Seaside

LAKE/RIVER FRONT
Celebration Hotel
Harborfront Inn
Lakeside Inn

WORKING FIREPLACES IN SOME ROOMS
Fairbanks House
Governors Inn
Josephine's
Lodge & Club at Ponte Vedra Beach

70

BIKING
Amelia Island
Anna Maria Island
Celebration
Knight's Island
Mount Dora
New Smyrna Beach
KITCHENS AVAILABLE IN ROOMS
Palm Island Resort
Song of the Sea
Turtle Beach Resort
24-HOUR ROOM SERVICE
Chesterfield Hotel
Four Seasons Resort, Palm Beach
Lodge & Club at Ponte Vedra Beach
Peabody Orlando Hotel
Naples Registry Resort
Ritz-Carlton Amelia Island
ART GALLERIES AND MUSEUMS
Delray Beach
Fort Lauderdale
Orlando
Palm Beach
St. Augustine
Winter Park
PLACES YOU DON'T REALLY NEED A CAR
Casa Monica Hotel
Celebration Hotel
Chesterfield Hotel
Colony Hotel & Cabana Club
Fairbanks House
Governors Inn
Harrington House
Josephine's
Lakeside Inn
Palm Island Resort
Park Plaza Hotel
Peabody Orlando Hotel
Riverside Hotel
Riverview Hotel
Song of the Sea

I Don't Know Much

We don't know much... and the pace of "everyday life" doesn't give us much luxury time to laze about and think about living and loving and how lucky we are. Make time on your next escape.

"I don't know much, but I know I love you, and that may be all I need to know." — *Aaron Neville*

"They talk about the dignity of work. Bosh. The dignity is in leisure." — *Melville*

"The way to love anything is to realize that it might be lost." — *Chesterton*

"A true relationship between a man and a woman is one in which the independence is equal, the dependence mutual, and the obligation reciprocal." — *Louis Anspacher*

"Today is unique, share it, do something wonderful with it . . . for it will never come again." — *Flavia*

"Love does not only exist in gazing at each other but in looking outward together in the same direction." — *Antoine de Saint-Exupery*

"The most thoroughly wasted of all days is that on which one has not laughed." — *Chamfort*

"One word frees us from all the weight and pain of life: That word is love." — *Sophocles*

FLORIDA'S ROMANTIC INLAND

**TALLAHASSEE
MOUNT DORA
WINTER PARK
ORLANDO
CELEBRATION
LAKE WALES**

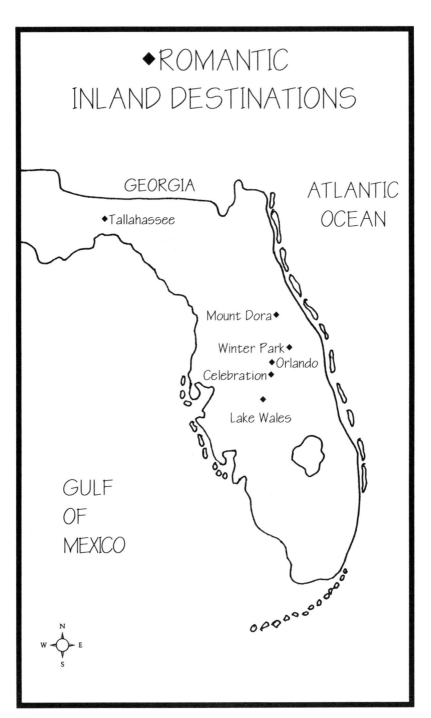

◆ROMANTIC
INLAND DESTINATIONS

GEORGIA

ATLANTIC
OCEAN

◆Tallahassee

Mount Dora◆

Winter Park◆
◆Orlando
Celebration◆
◆
Lake Wales

GULF
OF
MEXICO

N
W ◆ E
S

CHAPTER 13

A ROMANTIC ESCAPE TO TALLAHASSEE

AN OVERVIEW

The Tallahassee area is hilly and forested with fragrant pines. This quiet and dignified town in north Florida is the state's capital and the architecture in the Capitol Complex spans the centuries. Part of the Old Capitol was built before the Civil War but standing behind it is the New Capitol, a sleek 22-story skyscraper. Ancient oaks line many avenues and the parks are stunning in the spring when the azaleas are in bloom.

The charming Governors Inn is a comfortable and refined retreat just one block from the Capitol Complex. The two of you can settle in to a suite with a sleeping loft or a jetted tub. It can get chilly here in the winter and a suite with a fireplace (they supply the wood) is a warm winter choice.

An excellent restaurant and great jazz are right across the street and historical sights are nearby. There is no pool here and this definitely isn't a beach destination. However, the hilly streets and grassy parks are pleasant for quiet walks and romantic talks.

LODGING FOR LOVERS
THE GOVERNORS INN

Suites in this intimate and elegant inn are inviting and sophisticated quarters made for relaxing, sleeping, and taking it easy. A romantic restaurant is across the street.

A brick walkway leads to the etched glass and varnished wood doors of this elegant inn. This building was originally a 19th-century hardware store, and the architect kept the handsome exterior brick and did a fine job of incorporating the original and massive heart-of-pine beams into a country French interior.

Each room and suite is named for a different governor of Florida and each is uniquely decorated. All are handsomely furnished with a mix of antiques and reproductions—four-poster beds, writing desks, armoires. You'll find thick terry robes in the closet and your shoes shined if you leave them outside the door when you retire.

The standard rooms are on the small side but the appealing furnishings make them cozy and inviting retreats. However, the unusual suites are the real romantic draw here. No two are alike in shape or size. In the suites you'll find sky-lights, high ceilings, and charming little windows. Some have wood-burning marble fireplaces and circular stairways that lead up to a romantic loft bedroom. One unit has a sexy whirlpool tub. These suites are comfortable and well-appointed and inviting places to settle into.

Groupings of upholstered chairs and sofas are scattered around the spacious and warm, pine-paneled Florida Room. Guests gather here for complimentary cocktails in the early evening. Continental breakfast is served here in the morning but it's much more romantic to call down and have them bring it to your room so you can enjoy it in bed.

During the weekdays transportation from the airport is provided. Non-smoking rooms available. Children welcome. Check-out 12 noon. Romantic Packages. 40 rooms and suites. 209 S. Adams St., Tallahassee, 32301. Reservations: 800-342-7717. Tel: 850-681-6855. Fax: 850-222-3105. $129-$229.

A RESTAURANT FOR LOVERS
ANDREW'S 2ND ACT

Hidden downstairs in this New Orleans-style building is one of Tallahassee's finest restaurants. Settle into a quiet booth for a peaceful meal at this dark and romantic retreat. The cuisine is Continental and the grouper Cardinale, veal Oscar, and tournedos St. Laurent have been house specialties for years. Dishes prepared for two tableside include Caesar salad and a superb Steak Diane but even better are the tableside-prepared flaming desserts. It's a tough decision: sublime bananas foster or elegant cherries jubilee. Sunday brunch is a treat here. *No lunch weekends. 228 S. Adams St., 850-222-3444. $$-$$$.*

ROMANTIC THINGS TO DO HERE

In the spring when the azaleas are in bloom, don't miss the stunning 307-acre Maclay Ornamental Gardens *(3540 Thomasville Rd., 850-487-4556).* Come anytime for hiking, biking, and horseback riding.

Head to the LeMoyne Art Center *(125 N. Gadsen St., 850-222-8800)* for the current exhibit, the sculpture garden, and classical music.

Enjoy an evening of excellent jazz at Andrew's Bar and Grill *(228 S. Adams St., 850-222-3444).*

Dine romantically inside a restored 1920s house or outside under the oaks and enjoy superbly-prepared French cuisine at Chez Pierre *(1215 Thomasville Rd., 850-222-0936).*

For a great and graciously-served Italian meal go straight to Anthony's *(1950 Thomasville Rd., 850-224-1447).*

Catch a spectacular view of this pretty city. Take an elevator to the 22nd floor observatory atop the Florida State Capitol at Monroe Street.

ROMANTIC RADIO
Soft rock: 98.9FM   Jazz:100.9FM
ROMANTIC REMINDERS
What to Bring: Something warm in the winter. It can be chilly here.
Directions: I-10, exit 29. South on Monroe. Right on College. Left on Adams.

BUT SERIOUSLY FOLKS ...

A Magical Romantic Escape Doesn't Happen Like Magic

The truth is that whether you and your lover are escaping for a weekend or a few weeks, you have to do some work to make it work. Here are some hints to help you enjoy your escape a little bit more.

❑**Make sure you both agree on your "escape"** and chose your destination together. Make sure you both understand what there is to do there.

❑**Remember that very few mortals can leave a hectic and high-pressured pace and just "decide" to be relaxed, romantic, and walk barefoot in the sand.** Try to plan something the day before you leave—a leisurely dinner or a long evening walk—to get the wind-down process started before you leave.

❑**Give yourself the gift of time**—plenty of time for an unhurried departure and plenty of travel time to get where you are going. And, of course, the time to do whatever the two of you want to do after you've made your escape.

❑**You have the privilege of taking a special trip with the person you love very much.** The two of you belong to each other this trip. Not to the office, not to the kids, to no one but each other.

❑**Plan a "soft landing" for your return to "reality."** A dinner for two after you get home. The kids or phone calls or messages or mail or work can survive without you for another twelve hours or so.

CHAPTER 14

A ROMANTIC ESCAPE TO MOUNT DORA

AN OVERVIEW

You drive through fields and farm country to get to Mount Dora, a tiny lakeside town in central Florida. Orlando is only 45 minutes away but you feel as if you are in the middle of nowhere. The scenery is beautiful here and also quite unlike most people's idea of Florida. The land is vaguely hilly and densely covered with leafy green trees.

Mount Dora's romantic hideaway is the Lakeside Inn, built in 1883 and listed on the National Register of Historic Places. It's right on a lake and if either of you has ever spent a summer by a lake anywhere, this lovely inn will strike a nostalgic chord.

Just around the corner from the inn is a charming little town with a large number of antique stores, several art galleries, and about a dozen restaurants. You can walk everywhere along quiet, tree-lined streets. This is not a place to come for a lot of late-night activities. Restaurants close here by 9:00 p.m. during the week, somewhat later on weekends. When you tire of walking the town, there are boat trips and train rides to catch your fancy.

LODGING FOR LOVERS
THE LAKESIDE INN

Built in 1883 and overlooking a peaceful lake where you can canoe or take a boat ride, this nostalgic inn has a picturesque little town right around the corner and it's just a short walk to interesting antique shops and art galleries and a fine choice of restaurants.

Your grandparents or great-grandparents may have actually stayed here if they vacationed in Florida. White wicker rocking chairs line the inn's long veranda and a green lawn sweeps down to the large pool and serene Lake Dora. At sunset the lake reflects the spectacular colors of the evening sky and at night it catches the stars.

The rooms are in a cluster of wooden buildings which resemble over-size houses, painted pale yellow with steep gables and green-shingled roofs. Each of the 88 rooms is a slightly different shape and size. All have wonderfully high ceilings, are nicely painted or wallpapered, and have large closets (for those trunks full of fancy attire guests traveled with in the 1920s, when the inn was in its hey-day). Hallways creak here and bathrooms are comfortably old-fashioned.

The most romantic rooms are probably the extra-large lakefront rooms with giant picture windows that frame the water view but it's also romantic to stay on the second floor of the main building. Lake views here are further away but still good, and you can just walk downstairs to meals and the inn's large, inviting living room with a fireplace. For a romantic splurge, go for the private third-floor suite with a living room and separate bedroom, both with superb views of the lake.

The Beauclaire Dining Room is open for all meals plus brunch on Sunday and there is room service during regular meal hours. Tremain's Lounge has lively entertainment on weekends.

Pool, tennis courts, horseshoes, shuffleboard, croquet. Fee for canoes, boats, bikes, lake cruises. Some rooms with refrigerators. Non-smoking rooms available. Check-out 11:00 a.m. Romantic Packages. 88 rooms.100 N. Alexander St., Mount Dora, 32757. Reservations: 800-556-5016. Tel: 352-383-4101. Fax: 352-735-2642. Web: www.lakeside-inn.com. $90-$150.

A RESTAURANT FOR LOVERS
GOBLIN MARKET

The romantic setting here is the first floor of a quaint frame house. Tables are well-spaced in two dark and intimate rooms. Papered walls and shelves of books provide a cozy background for a long and splendid evening. The menu is eclectic and inventive. Try the crab bisque or the escargot or the wild mushroom tartare for starters. Then opt for the porcini-dusted veal or the bourbon-glazed pork tenderloin or the snapper seared with a caramelized onion crust. When the weather is agreeable, the outside courtyard in back is a romantic choice. Come Thursday to hear a gifted acoustic guitar player. *Reservations necessary. Closed Sun., Mon. 331-B Donnelly St., 352-735-0059. $$-$$$.*

ROMANTIC THINGS TO DO HERE

Stroll out to the end of the spacious dock at night. You'll hear loons, see a zillion stars, frequently catch spectacular thunderstorm light shows in the distance and sparkling firefly shows up close.

Hop into a seaplane and catch the scenery from the air. The little seaplane leaves right from the Lakeside Inn dock. Call Southwind Seaplane Tour *(Lakeside Inn dock, 800-611-3727).* For two people, the cost is $118 for 20 minutes, $138 for 30 minutes, and $170 for an hour.

See if you can spot an alligator after dark. Romantic? Well, you have to do it together in the dark. From the end of the dock look for a silent, slightly darker shape gliding silently in the water. Shine a flashlight; although it's a little scary when you make contact with those red eyes.

Take an old-fashioned horse-drawn carriage ride for two through downtown Mount Dora. Call Classic Carriages *(352-589-2555).*

Get a table for two and share a special "dinner for two" at the Palm Tree Grill *(351 Donnelly St., 352-735-1936).* Choose between a platter of shrimp scampi, lobster tail, and N.Y. steak or a seafood extravaganza. Or order separately and dine on some great Italian food.

Have a cafe au lait and browse through the many books at the inviting Dickens- Reed *(140 W. 5th St., 352-735-5950)* bookstore.

Go to a play together at the Ice House Theater (*1100 N. Unser St., 352-383-4616*). There's a play every month except July and August.

For a taste of Britain, drop by the Windsor Rose English Tea Room (*144 W. 4th Ave., 352-735-2551*) for authentic scones and pastries and also excellent sandwiches.

Board a 1920s-era railroad car for a scenic railroad ride. The Dora Doodlebug (*Alexander St. at 3rd Ave., 352-383-4368*) runs through hilly countryside, along the shore of Lake Dora, and into historic downtown Mount Dora. Fare is $8 per person.

Yellow ceiling fans spin lazily at elegant Ivy's (*439 N. Donnelly St., 352-383-4277*), where flowers grace the tables and the sesame-seared tuna, rack of lamb, and parmesan-encrusted veal chop are superb. It's definitely a romantic choice for dinner.

Head out to a winery for a tasting. Lakeridge Winery & Vineyards (*19239 US 27N., 352-394-8627*) in Clarmont is a pretty 45-minute drive away on winding roads around lakes and over small hills.

Spend the morning putt-putting around the lake in your own little run-about. Call Fun Boats (*Lakeside Inn, 352-735-2669*) to rent powerboats, pontoon boats, paddle boats, canoes, and chairboats. You can even boat to an Irish pub, O'Keefe's (*352-343-2157*).

Have fun sampling the wine flights (two ounces each of five different wines) for lunch Tuesday through Saturday and dinner Friday and Saturday at Shiraz (*301 Baker St., 352-735-5227*).

For an amazing assortment of wind accessories (kites, wind socks, flags), stop by Tierra Fina (*237 W. 4th Ave., 352-735-0334*).

ROMANTIC RADIO
Easy: 107.7FM   Oldies: 105.9FM
ROMANTIC REMINDERS
What to Bring: Even summer evenings can be cool here so bring a sweater.
Directions: 35 miles northwest of Orlando, off of Rt. 441. The Lakeside Inn provides excellent driving directions.

A VERY SPECIAL FLORIDAY

fresh orange juice in bed or on the beach

a morning stroll arm in arm

some shopping or snoozing in the morning sun

a back rub and a bath

a picnic in the pines - a loaf of bread, jug of wine, and thou

some splendor in the grass

an afternoon dip

an ice cream cone or two

some bubbly in a bubble bath

some fine food and flickering light

a dance around the floor

then tucked in bed together for the night

INEXPENSIVE ROMANTIC GIFTS

Wine — you can find terrific wines in bottles and half bottles for under ten dollars almost anywhere.

Flowers — buy cut flowers by the stem, rather than in an arrangement, and you can get beautiful bouquets for ten dollars or less at any florist. Or just get one perfect rose.

A Picture Frame — you can buy a fine-looking one in a K-Mart or a Walgreens's for just a few dollars. Add a special photo and it becomes a priceless gift.

Bath salts or bubble bath — a wonderful inexpensive gift you can enjoy together.

Candles — you can buy candles almost anywhere, and there are usually some on sale. Candles add immediate romance to a dinner or bath or even a midnight snack.

Books — all bookstores have bargain tables where you can purchase great books for a fraction of the original price.

Candy — you don't need a box of Godiva chocolate that takes two people to lift to show that you're sweet on your lover.

© 2000 by Pamela Acheson and Richard B. Myers from *The Best Romantic Escapes in Florida*

CHAPTER 15

A ROMANTIC ESCAPE TO WINTER PARK

AN OVERVIEW

In central Florida, just a few minutes northwest of downtown Orlando is the little college town of Winter Park, a peaceful enclave where the boughs of century-old oaks form canopies across quiet streets. Shops, art galleries, restaurants, and even a wonderful museum are on calm Park Avenue, a brick drive that runs alongside a lovely park.

The most romantic lodging choice is the Park Plaza Hotel. This restored inn adjoins one of the most romantic restaurants in town, and it is right on Park Avenue.

It's the whole relaxing experience, not so much the bits and pieces, that make it romantic to stay on Park Avenue. Since virtually everything is within easy walking distance, you won't need your car, so you won't have to deal with traffic, finding parking spots, or getting lost.

When you do feel like venturing out, more excellent restaurants and an art film dinner theater are just a short drive away.

LODGING FOR LOVERS
PARK PLAZA HOTEL

Built in the 1920s, this renovated two-story cross between a hotel and an inn is a comfortable and romantic spot to settle into. It is just steps away from restaurants, cafes, shops, and the peaceful park.

A profusion of tropical plants and flowers fill the wrap-around second floor balcony. Individually decorated rooms have richly patterned wallpapers, fancy moldings, oriental rugs, and hardwood floors. The smaller rooms are cozily romantic but if you plan to spend some time inside you'll probably want a Balcony Suite which comes with a King bed and a living room area plus a door to the balcony.

Order up the complimentary continental breakfast for two and enjoy it in bed or out on the little balcony (although it's communal, the plants keep most tables private). In winter, during a cold snap, sit by the fire in the lobby or stay under the covers and share a bottle of champagne. For a romantic restaurant, just walk downstairs to the Park Plaza Gardens for lunch or dinner or a great Sunday brunch (or have a romantic meal in your room—this restaurant provides room and bar service for the hotel from 11:00 a.m. to 11:00 p.m.).

Non-smoking rooms available. No children under 5. Check-out 12 noon. Romantic Packages. Proprietor: Sandra C. Spang. 27 rooms and suites. 307 S. Park Ave., Winter Park, 32789. Reservations: 800-228-7220. Tel: 407-647-1072. Fax: 407-647-4081. Web: www.parkplazahotel.com. $95-$200.

If you want to stay at a place with a pool . . .
THE LANGFORD RESORT HOTEL
Just a two-block walk from Park Avenue is this old-time family-owned resort hotel. Rooms and bathrooms are dated but there is a large pool in a lovely courtyard with tropical plants, a little spa where you can get therapeutic and aromatherapy massages (the two of you can also order up a massage in your room), and a bar with entertainment and dancing most nights. Ten "theme" rooms, which range from antebellum-southern (with a four-poster bed) to funky '60s are a bit quirky but more fun than the other rooms. *220 rooms, 66 with kitchens. 300 E. New England Ave. Tel: 407-644-3400. Fax 407-628-1952. $65-$105.*

RESTAURANTS FOR LOVERS

PARK PLAZA GARDENS

This quiet, dimly-lit oasis is particularly romantic at night. Tiny white lights twinkle in the boughs of full-size potted trees and the atmosphere is peaceful, refined, and never hurried. For a romantic beginning share an appetizer, such as the baked brie and apple napoleon. For entrees, the cedar plank roasted salmon, fire-roasted rack of lamb, and farfalle pesto with grilled shrimp are house favorites. The wine list is extensive. A pianist plays during dinner on weekends and during brunch on Sunday. *319 S. Park Ave., 407-645-2475. $$$.*

MAISON DES CREPES

Hidden back in an alleyway is this glass-walled little restaurant that is dark and intimate at night. There are several small dining rooms and you can share a chateaubriand or the Beef Wellington. The somewhat French menu includes stuffed artichokes, escargots, frogs legs, and bouillabaisse a la Marseillaise. Entree and dessert crepes are the house specialty. *348 N. Park Ave. 407-647-4469. $$-$$$.*

ROMANTIC THINGS YOU CAN WALK TO

To see enormous, beautifully romantic Tiffany glass murals and to read what must be the most delightfully amusing descriptive captions ever written, go to the Morse Museum (*445 N. Park Ave., 407-645-5311*). Be sure to walk through Tiffany's stunning 1893 chapel interior, painstakingly reassembled here, and an awesome sight.

Sneak out and buy your partner a diamond at the Park Promenade (*152 S. Park Ave., 407-644-7119*). They have estate jewelry, too.

Check out the delicate blown glass, whimsical tiles by Sophie, handcrafted jewelry, sculptures, and much more at fabulous Timothy's Gallery (*212 N. Park Ave., 407-629-0707*).

Walk to a boat trip around Lake Osceola with Winter Park Scenic Boat Tours (*Morse Blvd. at Lake Osceola, 407-644-4056*).

If you fell in love in college let a walk through the Rollins College campus stir up romantic memories. Go to a play or a concert or a game.

Listen to Michael Lamy croon Broadway show songs and play the piano in the back room at the Village Bistro *(326 S. Park Ave., 407-740-7573)* Tuesday through Saturday starting at 8:30.

Wander through the Nicole Miller boutique *(312 Park Ave., 407-628-0400)* for sexy cocktail dresses and a huge collection of her wonderfully zany neckties.

Check out the array of watches for men and women at Reynolds and Company Jewelers *(232 Park Ave., 407-645-2278)*. If you're in the market for something fancy at a really good price, ask to see their selection of estate watches.

For exceptionally delicious fruit smoothies, vegetarian sandwiches, fresh salads, and their tasty specialty, tuna salad with bulgar wheat tucked in a pita, head around the corner to the tiny Powerhouse Cafe *(111 E. Lyman Ave., 407-645-3616)*. Dine at a little table inside or take your order over to the park.

ROMANTIC STOPS A SHORT DRIVE AWAY

For a superb lunch or dinner go straight to stylish Antonio's *(611 S. Orlando Ave., 407-645-5523)*. The cuisine here is pure Italian—from the fresh Bufala mozzarella to the linguini alle vongole to the gamberoni Siciliana served with risotto.

Enjoy a decadent dessert, or light cuisine, or just a glass of wine, and see award-winning movies at the Enzian Theater *(1300 S. Orlando Ave., 407-629-1088)*.

Share an excellent chateaubriand prepared tableside in one of Nicole St. Pierre's *(1300 S. Orlando Ave., 407-647-7575)* four intimate dining rooms. Have a drink first in their upstairs bar which looks out to trees.

ROMANTIC RADIO
Easy: 107.7FM   Jazz: 103.1FM   Oldies: 105.9FM
ROMANTIC REMINDERS
What to Bring: People here are dressed in everything from suits to shorts.
Directions: I-4, exit 46. East on Lee Rd. to 17-92 and turn right. Go to Webster St. (1st light) and go left. Go to Park Ave. and turn right.

WHEN TO GO?

We asked hundreds of couples when is the best time to take a romantic escape in Florida. Here are just some of the answers.

"February. Even two or three days down here together gives us enough warmth to get through the winter back home."

"If you feel real life is fighting to pull the two of you apart."

"When you simply can't remember the last time that you just sat around and hugged each other."

"The best time? Any time you can."

"I don't know if it is the best time, but we always plan a weekend getaway to celebrate our wedding anniversary alone together. It's the best weekend of the year."

"Our whole life together is a romantic escape... in Florida or anywhere else."

"The best time for any romantic escape is when I can find someone crazy enough to go with me."

"Unquestionably the most romantic time for an 'escape' is when both of you are incredibly busy

and should be doing one hundred other things and you just say, 'Sorry' and go frolic somewhere together for a couple of days."

"The middle of the week, in the middle of the day, when everyone else is working, that's the time for romance and escape."

"October is Florida's most beautiful month and romance is always beautiful so I'd just say October."

"Right now."

"The best time for a romantic escape for us is when her parents go on a cruise and leave us the condo."

"What are you, crazy? Anytime."

"The best time for any romantic escape is when the kids are in school."

"After the Super Bowl and before the next football season starts. I think that's a week or so in May sometime."

"Well, let's see. Any day of the week that ends with 'y'."

"The summer. The weather is guaranteed to be great along the shore!"

CHAPTER 16

A ROMANTIC ESCAPE TO ORLANDO

AN OVERVIEW

When the two of you want to retreat from the world and settle into a sophisticated full-service hotel that you don't have to leave, head to the Peabody Orlando hotel. There's a complete spa, a superbly romantic restaurant, an Olympic-size swimming pool plus places to bask in the sun or sit in the shade, a poolside snack bar, tennis courts, an Italian bistro, a '50s-style dinner, a take-out deli, dancing, and four bars. It's close to Disney World but you'd never, ever know it.

This is an incredibly easy romantic escape if you live near a major city in the northeast. The hotel is just 20 minutes from the Orlando International Airport and there many flights daily from most major cities. This is also, of course, a great sophisticated retreat if you live in Florida.

If you do want to go off to see an Orlando Magic game or make a foray to Epcot (or even to see Mickey), the Peabody Orlando also makes a wonderfully romantic base for exploring Central Florida.

LODGING FOR LOVERS
THE PEABODY ORLANDO

Excellent service and an outstanding restaurant turn this posh high-rise hotel into a luxurious romantic hideaway.

This is a 27-story high-rise hotel with a lot of space around it and windows on the upper floors showcase the flat Florida landscape and spectacular lightning when a thunderstorm rolls in. Rooms are comfortable and decorated in soft restful colors. Executive King units have a spacious seating area.

You can keep the draperies drawn and stay in bed all day here or you can head down to the lobby to shop or out to the pool and tennis courts or go sit at a bar. Mallard's is the bar just off the lobby and in the back, tucked in between the columns, are two hidden seating nooks. The smaller one is perfect for lovers. Capriccio's bar is intimate and usually peaceful and quiet.

You can also settle into comfortable chairs in the atrium Lobby Bar and listen to a pianist during cocktail hour. Later in the evening there's music and dancing. In the afternoon stop by for tea. The hotel's signature ducks come and go from the lobby fountain every day (there's a twice-daily, duck-marching ceremony at 11:00 a.m. and 5:00 p.m.).

Dining choices abound at the Peabody, where there's even an all-night diner. For a romantic evening, get dressed up and head down to award-winning Dux or to the more casual Capriccio, which specializes in Northern Italian cuisine. For a delicious meal anytime day or night, get a table at the '50s-style B-Line Diner. It's open 24 hours and also has a take-out counter. You can also depend on 24-hour room service. The heated Olympic-size pool is in a large courtyard with shade trees and Coconuts Pool Bar. Various shops plus a Delta Airline and Avis Car Rental desk can be found in the lobby.

Pool, lighted tennis courts. Non-smoking rooms available. Check-out 12 noon. Excellent Romantic Packages. 871 rooms. 9801 International Dr., Orlando, 32819. Reservations: 800-PEA-BODY. Tel: 407-352-4000. Fax: 407-363-1505. Web: www.peabody-Orlando.com. $295-$420.

RESTAURANTS FOR LOVERS
DUX
All tables are romantic in this intimate, formal setting but the most romantic seats are in the corners. The innovative menu changes seasonally but includes such creations as tempura-fried escargots, roast sea scallops, a warm Florida lobster and rock shrimp salad, monk fish osso bucco with pancetta, pan-seared medallions of venison with chive ravioli, and a potato and black truffle torte plus desserts such as warm chocolate cake or a port-poached pear. Jackets are required for men. *Closed Sun. 407-352-4000, ext. 4550. $$$.*

CAPRICCIO
Dine lightly or have a full meal at this delightful northern Italian trattoria. Start with a bottle of Pinot Grigio and a traditional Caesar salad and then order two crispy pizzas and share them both. Or try the angel hair with tomatoes, or the penne with portobello mushrooms and sun-dried tomatoes, or the veal marsala. It can be clattery sitting close to the kitchen, so for a quiet table, ask to be near a window; it will be darker and more romantic there, too. Reservations are a must for the sumptuous Sunday brunch. *Closed Mon. 407-352-4000, ext. 4450. $$.*

ROMANTIC THINGS TO DO HERE
Relax together in a bubble bath. No, the tub isn't oversize, but two can fit and there's bath gel provided.

Pamper yourselves and spend a half-day together in the spa. Have deep-tissue Swedish, Shiatsu, and relaxation massages. Try an hour and a half, or even two. If you want, a massage therapist will come to your room.

Shop for bathing suits on your way in or out of the spa. This is a superb swimwear store (check out the sale rack).

ROMANTIC RADIO
Easy: 107.7FM   Oldies:105.9FM Country: 97FM
ROMANTIC REMINDERS
What to Bring: Dress-up clothes for Dux.
Directions: I-4, exit 28 to Beeline Expwy. Next exit north to International Dr.

ROMANTIC FLORIDA STUFF

Key Lime Pie

Spring Training

Small Friendly Towns

The Warmth

Water, Water Everywhere

The Seasons. Yes, The Seasons.

A-1-A

The Natural Beauty

Biking

CHAPTER 17

A ROMANTIC ESCAPE TO CELEBRATION

AN OVERVIEW

Celebration is southwest of downtown Orlando and northeast of Disneyworld. It's a planned community, created by Disney and designed to have all the best elements of an old-fashioned small town.

Celebration has the "picture-perfect" Disney touch, but indeed, the perfection is quite enviable. Lanes curve past pastel-painted houses, with shiny tin roofs and beautifully manicured front lawns. The hub of Celebration is a peaceful town square, set along the north side of a lake. Families and couples stroll along wide sidewalks, stopping at restaurants or shops, going to the bank or the post office or into the movie theater. If only real life could be this serene, you might wonder.

Overlooking the lake and right in town is the nostalgic and romantic Celebration Hotel. Visiting Celebration is a one-of-a-kind romantic escape. The town is more "perfect" than a town developed over time ever could be and it's a kick to be here. It may not feel quite like reality, but it's a fabulous escape.

LODGING FOR LOVERS
CELEBRATION HOTEL
You leave the real world behind when you stay at this nostalgic lakeside inn, with an old-fashioned town square right out the front door.

This sprawling three-story hotel is right on a lake and imbued with the style of 1920s Florida. It's a frame structure with dormer windows, clapboard siding, and tin roofs. Inside wainscotting and brick continue the old-Florida theme. In the lobby paddle ceiling fans turn lazily, and comfortable seating arrangements are well-spaced on the Brazilian walnut hardwood floors.

Almost all rooms and suites are on the second and third floors. They are painted pale yellow and furnished with handsome reproduction armoires and four-poster beds with big comforters to cuddle under. Many have balconies with stunning lake views.

The restaurant is open for breakfast only. It's an elegant affair, with linen tablecloths and fine table settings and glassware. Choose your ingredients at the omelet stand (or ask for eggs any style). The lighter (and less expensive) breakfast includes just the cold buffet. In the evening, guests gather around the lobby bar, with its stunning mural of Florida wildlife. Weekends, a pianist often entertains.

Sets of double doors open out from the lobby to a long veranda overlooking an incredibly peaceful lake. You could spend hours here in the comfortable rocking chairs. Or walk over to the adjacent pool and have a swim and catch some sun. For a real treat, head around the corner to the private outdoor whirlpool with a view of the lake and sky. When you feel like lunch or dinner or a stroll through town or a walk around the lake, just head out the door. Bear in mind that this is a family-oriented town and if there is an evening event for children in the square, there might be more children than normal around.

Pool, exercise room. Golf, fitness nearby. Non-smoking rooms available. Children welcome. Check out 11:00 a.m. Romantic Packages. 115 units. 700 Bloom St., Celebration, 34747. Reservations: 888-499-3800. Tel: 407-566-6000. Fax: 407-566-1844. Web: www.celebrationhotel.com. $185-$470.

A RESTAURANT FOR LOVERS
COLUMBIA RESTAURANT

The most romantic tables are in the alcove in the back or along the two-story arched windows that frame this popular restaurant, a sister of the original Columbia in Ybor City. You might start by sharing a pitcher of sangria. Then order some tapas or their signature black bean soup. Aromatic seafood paella is the house specialty and a romantic dish to share. Tables are outside, too. *649 Front St., 407-566-1505. $$-$$$.*

ROMANTIC THINGS TO DO HERE

Take a carriage ride through town Friday or Saturday evening between 6:00 and 10 p.m. Catch it across from Cafe D'Antonio's.

For some of the finest Italian cuisine around, make a reservation at Cafe D'Antonio's *(691 Front St., 407-566-2233)*.

Follow the path that goes around the lake, stopping along the way at a bench to talk and take in the view.

Dine on their famous Arizona salad or wood-fired filet mignon or barbecue St. Louis pork ribs at the Front Street Grill *(721 Front St., 407-566-1141)*. Save room for the strawberry shortcake.

Share a pastry and some coffee in the courtyard at Barnie's Coffee and Tea shop *(715-B Bloom St., 407-566-1284)*.

Be sure to stop in White's Books and Gifts *(715-C Bloom St., 407-566-1007)* for a great selection of books, greetings cards, and gifts.

Step back to the '50s with cheesy macaroni, meatloaf, or their truly retro Cafe Casserole at Max's Cafe *(701 Front St., 407-566-1144)*.

ROMANTIC RADIO
Jazz: 103.1FM Easy: 107.7FM Oldies: 105.9FM Country: 97FM
ROMANTIC REMINDERS
What to Bring: Casual clothes and yourselves are about all you'll need.
Directions: Toll Rd. 417, exit 1. Take Celebration Ave. to Sycamore St. Turn left. Drive to Front St. Turn right. Turn left at Bloom St.

WHAT IS THE AUTHORS' FAVORITE ESCAPE?

The inevitable question for us at any book signing or during any interview is: "Well, of all these destinations which is your favorite romantic escape?"

The answer is "All of the escapes in this book and its companion, *More of the Best Romantic Escapes in Florida*, are our favorites." That may sound like the politically correct answer, but it is also the truth.

Which escape becomes our "favorite" depends on what has been happening in our lives. If we've been chained to our desks for weeks dealing with deadlines, then a perfect romantic escape might be the elegant Chesterfield, with lots of restaurants and nightlife nearby. Or the Registry, where we can enjoy the beach, fine dining, be pampered at the Spa, and dance the night away at the disco without leaving the property.

If we've just finished a six-week authors' tour and been in a different city every day, then the perfect romantic escape might be Turtle Beach Resort where we have our own hot tub and our own kitchen and can cook what we like or have a delicious meal delivered from Ophelia's. Or it might be Palm Island Resort where we can dine when we want and live in a bathing suit.

The point is that any couples' "perfect romantic escape" may be different from one month to the next. It is why this book gives you 24 very different destinations that share one common ingredient, romance!

— P.A. and R.B.M.

CHAPTER 18

A ROMANTIC ESCAPE TO LAKE WALES

AN OVERVIEW

Lake Wales is pretty much in the center of central Florida. The town is well south of Disneyworld and in between Tampa to the west and Vero to the east. Lake Wales is "out of the loop" in terms of the Interstates and being there is close to really being absolutely in the middle of nowhere. The town itself is very tiny and there's not much to do there (although there is now a small mall, some restaurants, and even a movie theater).

Outside of this town, and even more remote, is the incomparable Chalet Suzanne Restaurant and Country Inn. It's set in rolling countryside, along a tiny lake. When the two of you want comfortable seclusion at a small inn in the country with formal dining, there's nothing more romantic than elegant Chalet Suzanne. It's an exquisite getaway and the perfect venue for a relaxing, indulgent, and romantic stay. Do nothing, or walk around the lake, or play croquet, or stay in bed all day. Bring books to read. This is one of the few places left where you can really get away from it all.

LODGING FOR LOVERS
CHALET SUZANNE

Chalet Suzanne Restaurant & Country Inn is an extremely peaceful "hide-out" for lovers. You can relax and do nothing in comfort. It's refined and yet ever-so-slightly whimsical.

This celebrated inn is on a 70-acre estate with exquisitely manicured grounds, a small lake, and its very own little grass airstrip. Thirty unique rooms are clustered together in an architectural jumble of spires and steeples, little balconies, gabled roofs, and arched doorways. It may sound odd but it works. Each room is unique here. They come in all sizes and shapes and are beautifully and individually decorated with a mix of antique and reproduction furniture, photographs and paintings, porcelain figurines, old clocks, and fresh flowers. Some have window seats or jetted tubs. The honeymoon suite has a dumbwaiter so that meals can be delivered without disturbing the newlyweds.

For such a little place, this is a remarkably complete resort. You can swim in the pool, spend hours wandering about in the tiny antique shop, read in the shade, walk down to the lake, go sit in the gazebo and watch for neat little rabbits, take a tour through the delightful soup "factory" where they actually make and can Chalet Suzanne soups, buy a ceramic dish from an in-residence ceramic artist, or shop in the little gift shop.

Although many come here just for the weekend, this is actually a beautifully romantic spot to head to for longer, especially if you want to spend a lot of time not doing much of anything.

Golf, tennis, sky-diving, and therapeutic massage can be arranged in 24 hours or less. This is definitely a place where the innkeeper makes the difference. Her mother-in-law may have invented this wonderful spot, but it is definitely Vita Henshaw who makes it work now.

Pool, croquet, horseshoes, antique shop, ceramic shop, gift shop. Non-smoking rooms available. Children are welcome. Check-out 11:00 a.m. Romantic Packages. 30 units. Innkeeper: Vita Henshaw. 3800 Chalet Suzanne Dr., Lake Wales, 33859. Reservations: 800-433-6011. Tel: 863-676-6011. Fax: 863-676-1814. Web: www.chaletsuzanne.com. $159-$229.

A RESTAURANT AND BAR FOR LOVERS
CHALET SUZANNE RESTAURANT

The Chalet Suzanne restaurant is open for breakfast, lunch, and dinner. There are a number of dining rooms but the hexagonal one overlooking the lake is probably the most romantic. A windowfront table for two looks out right over the peaceful little lake and in the daytime you might see turtles swimming about. The tables are set with a whimsical assortment of china. Be sure to take a look.

The two of you can take a morning walk or sleep and then head to a delightfully late breakfast (served until 11:00 a.m). The full breakfast includes eggs and sausage and irresistibly delicious thin little pancakes (just go for it when they tempt you with new little stacks of these).

Your first night here you are offered the complete Chalet Suzanne six-course signature dinner, but after that it's a la carte. The cuisine is on the rich side here and if you are staying a few days and want other choices, just let Mrs. Henshaw know. The dining room is quiet and refined and most men wear jackets at dinner. Friday and Saturday dine to the soft and lovely music of the piano. Breakfast, lunch, and dinner can be brought to your room if you prefer. Dinners are expensive, so be sure to check out the combined room/meal plans available. *$$$.*

CHALET SUZANNE BAR

Step into this tiny little bar for a before-dinner drink. If no one's around, just pull the bell. Bloody Marys are outstanding here. Carl Henshaw painted the marvelous mural of the marching drummers.

WINE DUNGEON

Head down the stairs to the mini-wine-tasting in the tiny Wine Dungeon from 5:30 to 7:30 p.m. There is barely enough room for the two of you.

ROMANTIC RADIO
Easy: 94.9FM   Jazz: 94.1FM   Classical: 90FM
ROMANTIC REMINDERS
What to Bring: Something a little dressy for dinner.
Directions: I-4, exit 23. South 20 mi. on Rt 27 to Chalet Suzanne Rd. Turn left and go 1-1/2 mi. to entrance on right. There's a 2450' grass airport and you can charter a plane from Tampa or Orlando.

101

ROMANTIC MONEY SAVERS

The best things in life may not be free, but certainly some of the most romantic things in life do not have to be expensive.

⌘You can have a bottle of Moet & Chandon and some pate and crackers in a hotel dining room for somewhere around $200...or you can also bring your own bottle of Chandon, some vegetarian pate, and some crackers and have them on your balcony under the stars or in your bathtub for about $20.

⌘After-dinner drinks in a sophisticated lounge or club are certainly romantic and a couple of libations each should run around $36 with tip....or you can pack your own little bottles of cognac or Perrier and enjoy them in bed or walking on a beach for about $6 with no tip.

⌘You can have your inn or resort make a picnic lunch for about $25...or you can find a deli and make your own for about $10.

⌘You can design and enjoy the wonderful day at the spa that you've always dreamed about for a few hundred dollars...or you can give each other a special day at your own private "spa" for next-to-nothing.

⌘You can extract anything you might ever want from your mini-bar at the usual mini-bar prices......or you can bring some of this stuff with you, at supermarket prices.

⌘You can order breakfast from room service...or bring fresh fruit and a bottle of sparkling water for breakfast in bed.

⌘Remember that a single perfect rose waiting to greet your love can be as romantic as all the flowers in the world.

TAKE A TRAIN

If you are coming to Florida from the northeast, try the train. For 20 hours, the landscape of the east coast rolls peacefully by. Before you say "20 hours, no way" – stop and think. Twenty hours together in a private compartment with a bed and no phones, and nothing to interrupt you.

In the daylight you see towns go by, including towns you thought no longer existed, with a little main street with a one-floor hardware store and not much else. The train goes by beautiful old houses and through miles and miles of forest and undeveloped land.

Service on this leg of Amtrak isn't exactly flawless, but there is a way to make this a wonderfully romantic adventure. However, don't do this unless both of you like the idea of camping, like to picnic, and you both truly like the idea of being unreachable for 20 hours.

The only compartments conducive to romance are the Deluxe Bedrooms in the Viewliner Sleeping Cars. At night – or whenever you want – the couch pulls out into a bed and a bunk pulls down from the ceiling. Two people can sleep in the bed if you like sleeping entwined (it's a cozy 3' x 6') and one of you can always go to the upper bunk for some serious shut-eye. There's also a little room with a toilet that is also a full shower, with good water pressure and nice hot water.

There is a dining car but don't even THINK of eating the food. Well, breakfast is okay, if you must, but the atmosphere in the dining car is not exactly romantic, and the service couldn't be much worse. So bring your own picnic with you. If you bring your food you can have a nice civilized dinner sitting across from each other in your compartment watching the world go by. Share a large bottle of water or a fine wine and dine on whatever the two of you like best – get a selection of gourmet salads, some cold chicken, chunks of cheeses, a loaf of French bread, and grapes or apples. Or get thick sandwiches from your local deli. Keep it all in a disposable styrofoam container that you can leave behind. You can eat whatever you didn't finish for the next day's lunch. (Complimentary coffee and packaged pastries or cookies are available.)

The attendant will come and put your bed up or down but not necessarily when you want, so do it yourself. It's easy to do and nice to be in charge, especially on this train. In fact, the only way to do this trip and make it fun and romantic is if you stay in charge.

With all these warnings, why take the train? It's very relaxing to slow down and do almost nothing for 20 hours. It's even more relaxing when you simply can't do anything, except sleep, take naps, read, play cards, talk, or think while you watch the scenery drift by. The noise of the wheels against the track and the regular rhythmic motion are soothing and peaceful. But you have to be happy to be out of touch.

What to bring: if you're a water-nut, bring your own (the train water is drinkable but not delicious). Luggage is inaccessible if you check it and not particularly easy to get at during the trip if you stow it in the roomy space above you, so pack a little bag with what you'll need while on board (toiletries, books, glasses). And dress comfortably.

Reservations: Amtrak, 800-872-7245. The round-trip price is similar to two nights of lodging plus airfare for two.

FLORIDA'S ROMANTIC WEST COAST

SEASIDE
ANNA MARIA ISLAND
SIESTA KEY
KNIGHT'S ISLAND
SANIBEL
NORTH NAPLES

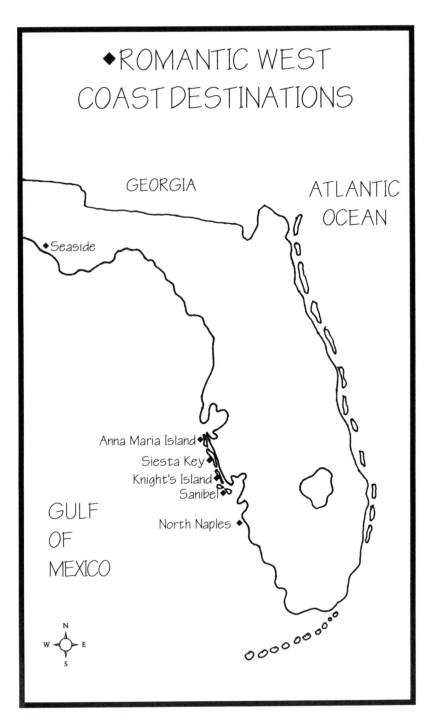

◆ROMANTIC WEST COAST DESTINATIONS

GEORGIA

ATLANTIC OCEAN

◆Seaside

Anna Maria Island◆

Siesta Key◆

Knight's Island◆

Sanibel◆

GULF OF MEXICO

North Naples ◆

N
W ◇ E
S

CHAPTER 19

A ROMANTIC ESCAPE TO SEASIDE

AN OVERVIEW

Improbably located on an isolated stretch of Florida's panhandle is a remarkable planned community known as Seaside. It's evocative of Nantucket or Martha's Vineyard or even Key West (and if you saw "The Truman Show," you'll recognize it; the Jim Carey movie was shot here).

This is an astonishing beachside cluster of white picket fences and brick walkways, of little pastel-painted clapboard cottages and wrap-around porches—an 80-acre celebration of creative architectural response to a strict set of design codes.

Everything in this casual but sophisticated community is within walking distance. It's very relaxing and people stroll about here. There are antique shops, art galleries, restaurants, boutiques, a bookstore, a wine bar, and a great little market. Walkways lead down to a half-mile stretch of gorgeous beach. For an enchanting romantic escape in Seaside, check yourselves into Josephine's French Country Inn, where you'll also find the best restaurant in town.

LODGING FOR LOVERS
JOSEPHINE'S

This elegant bed and breakfast is romantic and relaxing. The two of you can spend hours in your comfortable room in front of the fire or walk to sophisticated restaurants and shops and also to the beach.

A gate in a white picket fence marks the inviting entrance to Josephine's French Country Inn. The building is designed in the manner of a classic Georgian plantation, with imposing two-story columns, stately chimneys at each end, and wide verandas off both floors.

Each unit is different but all are nicely decorated with a mix of antique and reproduction furniture. Rooms have a little kitchen alcove with a sink, a microwave, and a small refrigerator and most have working fireplaces. The spacious suites are next to the main building and have a living room, a dining area, a separate bedroom, a full kitchen, and a working fireplace. Two of the suites also have whirlpool tubs. The most romantic choices are the two suites with views of the Gulf. A full gourmet breakfast in included in the rate.

This is a place to come to relax. You can walk everywhere. Spend your days at the gorgeous beach where the sand is dazzling white and the Gulf is a sheer Caribbean aquamarine. Or wander about the small town. There are often scheduled events held in the amphitheater in the village green. Despite the sophistication of Seaside, dress is casual here and the two of you can pack light.

Smoking outside only. No children. Check-out 11:00 a.m. Romantic Packages. 9 units (7 with fireplaces). Innkeeper: Sean Herbert. 101 Seaside Ave., (Mail address: P.O. Box 4767), Seaside, 32459. Reservations: 800-848-1840. Tel: 850-231-1940. Fax: 850-231-2446. Web:www.josephinesfl.com. $135-$240.

About two-thirds of the houses in the community are available for rent, including some honeymoon cottages right on the beach. Contact **Seaside Cottage Rental Agency** (*800-277-8696, www.seasidefl.com*) if you are interested.

A RESTAURANT FOR LOVERS
JOSEPHINE'S
This romantic restaurant is in the small and intimate, 10-table dining room of Josephine's French County Inn. A fire burns in the fireplace in all but the warmest months. The service in this enchanting spot is superb. Dine on fresh local seafood or their "InnFamous" crab cakes or a tender grilled filet or rack of lamb. There are also nightly specials. Incorporated in the cuisine are the organic vegetables, herbs, and edible flowers the owners grow at their farm. *Reservations necessary. Open Fri. and Sat. 101 Seaside Ave., 850-231-1939. $$-$$$.*

ROMANTIC THINGS TO DO HERE
Rent a kayak from Cabana Man (*George's Gorge, 850-231-5046*).

Have a custom-blend of bath oils created just for the two of you. Talk to the staff at Patchouli's (*Four Corners, 850-231-1447*).

Create a picnic for the beach from the gourmet selections at the marvelous Modica Market (*Central Sq., 850-231-1214*).

Stop in for an evening of jazz and blues at Bud & Alley's popular rooftop bar (*Cinderella Circle, 850-231-5900*).

Have a photograph taken of the two of you embracing on the beach in the glorious Florida sunset. Call Seashore Portraits (*850-231-5755*).

Share a glass of wine and some cheese at Fermentations Wine Bar (*25 Central Sq., 850-231-0167*). Choose from over 40 wines by the glass. Go to a tasting the first Friday and middle Wednesday of every month.

Try an Italian ice at Cafe Spiaggia (*2236 Hwy. 38, 850-231-1297*).

ROMANTIC RADIO
Easy: 95 FM Country: 102FM Oldies: 1450AM
ROMANTIC REMINDERS
What to bring: Sunscreen, a sweater for nighttime stargazing.
Directions: I-10, Exit 14. Go south on Rt. 331 to Rt. 98. Turn left (east) on Rt. 98. Go right (south) on Rt. 283 to Rt. 30A. Turn left.

A FEW TIME-TESTED ROMANTIC SURPRISES

Mail your lover a love letter or a love poem that will arrive before you do and be waiting when you check in.

Arrange for a bouquet of balloons, or a box of candy, or a favorite bottle of wine to be waiting in the room when you open the door.

Send ahead a photo album of your own pictures and some other personal "stuff" to reminisce and laugh about and ask that it be set out on a table in your room just before you arrive.

Have a gift-wrapped present delivered to your lover in your room, or to the pool, or to your table at dinner.

If there is live music wherever the two of you are headed, secretly arrange "your song" to be played sometime during your evening.

Ask to have your bed made up with satin sheets.

Arrange for a bouquet of flowers to be hidden in the shower. Or a ring to be under the pillow.

Make plans for a special room service presentation that is delivered unexpectedly.

CHAPTER 20

A ROMANTIC ESCAPE TO ANNA MARIA ISLAND

AN OVERVIEW

Remarkably peaceful Anna Maria Island lies just northwest of Sarasota on the Gulf of Mexico and boasts a seven-mile-long spectacular beach rimmed with tall and graceful Australian pines, some as high as 60 feet.

When you want to escape to one of the most enchanting getaways in Florida, just head to Anna Maria Island and the exquisitely romantic Harrington House, which is much more than a bed and breakfast. It's right smack on the beach and, remarkably, within walking distance of one of the state's very finest restaurants.

This is a place to come when the two of you want to spend days in bare feet, napping under a tree with a book in your lap, taking a dip in the pool and then another in the Gulf, biking around, and walking to a beach bar for lunch. One, some, or even every evening, you can put on something a little fancy, and walk on the beach, shoes in hand, to the intimate and immensely enjoyable Beach Bistro for an elegant and romantic dinner.

LODGING FOR LOVERS
HARRINGTON HOUSE

At this delightful beachfront bed and breakfast complex, your days are measured in large, romantic, relaxing chunks: late sleeps, long naps, lingering beach walks, leisurely dining, and nightcaps by the fire.

The entrance here is outstanding. A narrow path leads through tall trees and fragrant tropical flowers to a simple arched doorway. As you pass under the arch and into a little outdoor courtyard the world behind slips away and you feel as if you've actually crossed a magic threshold.

Rooms are in four buildings. If you want to be in a traditional bed and breakfast, choose the three-story main house, a frame building dating from 1925. Seven rooms are individually decorated with a mixture of furnishings, nicely wallpapered or painted, and some have beds facing directly out to the Gulf so the two of you can actually lie in bed and take in the view. Four rooms are in the Spangler Beach House, two houses away. Perhaps the most romantic choice is the Huth Beach House. Here four rooms are luxuriously furnished and have fireplaces. The Beach Bistro is next door and they'll even serve you dinner on your outside terrace! Another romantic choice is the tiny Honeymoon Cottage with a pink, heart-shaped jetted tub. All units have a balcony or patio, a TV/VCR, and a little fridge.

In the cozy living room of the main house, comfortable couches are arranged around a wood-burning fireplace. Floor-to-ceiling shelves hold books and video tapes. There's a menu for every restaurant within about 20 miles, popcorn in the early evening and, always, a plate of just-baked chocolate chip cookies. There are tables for two in the charming breakfast rooms. Outside is a good-size pool and beyond that the seven-mile beach. The specialness of the place and the caring attitude of the innkeepers make this experience wonderfully romantic. If you want something, or want something arranged, just ask.

Pool, bikes, kayaks. Smoking outside only. No children under 13. Check-out 11:00 a.m. 16 units. Romantic packages. Innkeepers: Jo and Frank Davis. 5626 Gulf Dr., Holmes Beach, Anna Maria Island, 34217. Tel: 941-778-5444. Fax: 941-778-0527. Web: www.harringtonhouse.com. $129-$249.

RESTAURANTS FOR LOVERS

BEACH BISTRO

One of the many great things about staying at the Harrington House is that, depending on where your room is, you are just a short walk (or a one-minute drive) or right next to this romantic and absolutely wonderful award-winning restaurant. It's built right on the beach with wall-to-wall windows that show off the view, but it really wouldn't matter if this place didn't have windows. You come for the exceptional quality and preparation of the food and the unobtrusively fine service. The menu is interesting and original. You can't go wrong, but the lobsterscargots, the lobster cakes, the scampi Chardonnay, the roast duck, and the tenderloin with cognac and pepper demi-glace are outstanding. Entrees come in regular and "lighter portions," so you can either eat lightly or try more items. Chocolate truffle terrine and key lime pie are superb here but the warmed bananas and berries in a cinnamon-dusted crepe is unbeatable. *Reservations necessary. No lunch. 6600 Gulf Dr., 941-778-6444. $$-$$$.*

BISTRO AT ISLAND'S END

Luckily for everyone, Beach Bistro owner Sean Murphy decided to open a second restaurant on Anna Maria Island. This one's a bit more casual (although it still has tablecloths) and a bit more whimsical, from the bright turquoise exterior trim to the airy ceiling decor to the laid-back, highly original cuisine. Try the superb fries with mango tomato ketchup, the Beastro Burger with apple-smoked cheddar, Mo's BLT (on grilled focaccia), the "Better than any Frenchman's" Onion Soup, or the superb pizza that combines Italian sausage, roasted peppers, and hoisin sauce. Hungrier diners can choose from such specialities as a rich seafood bouillabaisse, an outstanding filet mignon, tasty tempura shrimp, or grilled fresh salmon. Don't be afraid of the maple syrup and check out the wood carvings. *No lunch. 10101 Gulf Dr., 941-779-2444. $$.*

ROMANTIC THINGS TO DO HERE

Walk to the Sandbar Restaurant *(100 Spring Ave., 941-778-0444)* for lunch and have a lobster sandwich and a cold soda or beer on their expansive outdoor deck or step inside to the air-conditioned dining room with ocean views from both the tables and the handsome bar.

Head over on bikes to the end of the fishing pier on the east side of the island and see a unique view of faraway Tampa.

Rent a pontoon boat and explore the bay. Call Cortez Watercraft Rentals *(941-792-5263)* and spend the morning out on the water. Half day rentals are $100, full days are $150, both plus fuel and tax.

Pick out a sexy camisole or some slinky pants at the Beach Style Boutique *(10010 Gulf Dr., 941-778-4323)* or buy candles, housewares, or an upscale t-shirt.

Relax on a sailboat cruise at sunset time. Spice Sailing Charters *(Galati Yacht Basin, 941-778-3240)* will take just the two of you for a two-and-a-half-hour cruise. Or go on a half-day sail around Tampa Bay and out into the Gulf of Mexico. The "four person minimum" price is quite reasonable for two people. Bring your own beer or wine.

Dine for brunch or dinner in the casually romantic Sign of the Mermaid *(9707 Gulf Dr., 941-778-9399)*, cozily set in a tiny old Florida house.

Browse around the unusual shops in Bay View Plaza *(101 S. Bay Blvd.)*, on the east side of the island across from the fishing pier.

If you like to be alone together in a crowd, take the Cortez Lady cruise *(Cortez Rd. at bridge, 941-761-9777)* to Egmont Key, three miles away. The boat leaves Tuesday, Thursday, Saturday, and Sunday at 1:00 p.m. Tickets are $25 and it's wise to make reservations.

Thrill yourselves with a parasail ride. A Fun & Sun Parasail *(Bridge St., 941-795-1000)* will take you up for a memorable "sail!"

ROMANTIC RADIO
Easy 88.1FM   Jazz: 94.1FM   Classical: 90FM
ROMANTIC REMINDERS
What to Bring: Casual clothes plus something casually smart for the bistros. Snacks for your fridge. A bottle of bubbly for star watching on the beach. *Directions: I-75, exit 42. Go west 11 mi. on Rt. 64 to Rt. 789 (Gulf Dr.) and turn right (north). Be sure to stay on Gulf Dr. (it twists here and there).*

SHARING

Whether the two of you are sharing your lives together or just a few footprints in the sand, try sharing some of the ideas below on your next romantic escape.

Share your meals. Order foods you both want to taste or try, and share your choices. It can be breakfast in bed, a picnic lunch, or a special dinner. Or order meals made tableside for two, like Caesar salad or chateaubriand or cherries jubilee.

Share a book. Take turns reading aloud to one another from a book you'll both enjoy together, or get two copies of the same book and read them together, separately.

Share "back-to-back" massages. Give each other a half-hour massage after a tough day of relaxing and before your evening bath or shower together.

Share a sensuous shampoo session. Or dry each other's hair. If one partner is hirsutely challenged, then a scalp massage is nice.

Share a carafe of wine. Or a bottle of mineral water. Or a pitcher of juice. Pour for each other.

Share some silence together. During a long walk on the beach, or while on a bench in the park, a canoe on a lake, or just silently holding each other in bed.

Share paying or signing for everything. It doesn't matter whose money actually is paying. Share the joy of the act of "buying" things for each other.

© *2000* by Pamela Acheson and Richard B. Myers from *The Best Romantic Escapes in Florida*

THE MOST ROMANTIC FROM A TO Z

Afterhours Dancing: Leopard Lounge
Brunch: Naples Registry
Coffee: O'Kane's
Dinner: Beach Bistro
Entrance: Harrington House and Song of the Sea
Fireplaces: Fairbanks House and Governors Inn
Gallery: Morse Museum
Hot Tubs: Turtle Beach Resort
Italian Restaurant: Renato's
Jazz: Andrew's Bar and Grill
Kayaking: The Registry
Library: Chesterfield
Moonlit Walk: Palm Island Resort
Nightclub: Club Zanzibar
Open Air Lunch: Toni and Joe's
Piano During Dinner: Portofino
Quiet Bar: Beach Bistro
Room Service Menu: Four Seasons Resort,
Palm Beach
Sexiest Bedroom: Riverside Hotel
Two-Person Bar: Chalet Suzanne
Understated Elegance: Chesterfield
Views: Ritz-Carlton Amelia Island
Wine List: Peabody Dux
X-rated Ceiling: Leopard Lounge
Yellowfin Tuna: Beech Street Grill
Ziti: Vincenzo's

CHAPTER 21

A ROMANTIC ESCAPE TO SIESTA KEY

AN OVERVIEW

Siesta Key is a long, slender barrier island just east of Sarasota and has good shelling beaches facing the Gulf of Mexico. It's primarily a residential island and the scenery along the main road switches back and forth from gated private driveways with manicured hedges and hidden mansions to the occasional mid-rise condo set amidst an expanse of carefully-tended lawn.

Tucked along the edge of the peaceful Intracoastal Waterway on the very narrow and residential (and non-trafficky) south end of the island is tiny and romantic Turtle Beach Resort, a cluster of funky cottages, each with a complete kitchen and its own private outdoor hot tub.

There are hammocks slung here and there in the tropical greenery. There's a pool overlooking the waterway and a little dock with canoes and rowboats. The Gulf and a great beach are a three-minute walk away. Right next door is one of Sarasota's most romantic restaurants. What more could you ask for?

117

LODGING FOR LOVERS
TURTLE BEACH RESORT

This romantic cluster of cottages, each with a private outdoor hot tub, is a one-of-a-kind spot. It's casual and funky and feels a bit like Key West or the Caribbean.

This delightful escape is right on the water, on an offshoot of the Intracoastal Waterway. It looks impossibly small when you drive up to it, and indeed, cottages are in a compact cluster, but they are extremely private inside. Studios and one- and two-bedroom units have VCRs and full kitchens, and each also has its own very private hot tub.

Things are laid-back here. Cottages are casually decorated and each has a loosely-followed theme. The Southwestern Cottage features a Mexican tile shower. Country French has a four-poster bed. The Country Cottage is sort of "Pier 1" country. Most have some sort of water view and several cottages are right on the water.

The grounds are dense with tropical greenery. There's a heated pool overlooking the Intracoastal Waterway, hammocks big enough for two, and several little docks. The water views are superbly peaceful.

It's incredibly easy to be here. You have a full kitchen, but if you don't want to cook, just walk next door to Ophelias's on the Bay. It's one of the best restaurants in the Sarasota area and they'll even deliver a romantic dinner right to your cottage! You can walk to the most empty beach on Siesta Key in three minutes and swim or sit in the sun or go shelling. You can easily walk to several very casual restaurants. You can take a rowboat or canoe to a very private strip of sand.

It is the innkeepers here who really make a difference and if you want something special, just ask. Beware that children are welcome and could be heard playing outside in such a compact place.

Pool, dock, canoes, rowboats, fishing poles, bikes. Maid service additional. Check-out 10:00 a.m. Romantic Packages. 10 cottages. Innkeepers: Gail and Dave Rubinfeld. 9049 Midnight Pass Rd., Siesta Key, 34242. Tel: 941-349-4554. Fax: 941-918-0203. Web: www.turtlebeachresort.com. $135-$255.

118

RESTAURANTS FOR LOVERS

OPHELIA'S ON THE BAY

This romantic and elegant gem is right on the water, right next door to the Turtle Beach Resort. Reserve a table along the wall of windows in one of the two romantically-lit dining rooms or on the outside deck and gaze at the peaceful, placid waterway. If you are there at twilight, watch the colors of the water change and look for dolphins swimming along. Start with baked oysters with asiago cheese sauce or marinated Gulf shrimp or grilled sea scallops or share Ophelia's Sampler, which is a sampling of all three. For entrees, the filet mignon with shitake mushroom gravy, shrimp scampi, and pork tenderloin are excellent choices. *Dinner only. 9105 Midnight Pass Rd., 941-349-2212. $$-$$$.*

SUMMERHOUSE

For a romantic setting, this has to be one of the best anywhere. The dining room walls are all solid glass, floor-to-ceiling; invisible windows that define the edges of a forest. Everywhere you look there are trees and more trees, deftly lit at night. A series of angles means that most tables are windowside and diners are treated to a stunning, awesome view of a tropical mix of trees, plants, and stately trunks that come right up to the glass. A pianist plays nightly and the air is rich with romantic piano music. It's a true pleasure, in an airy, intimate, romantic setting like this, to find out that the cuisine here is excellent, too. Try the shitake mushrooms and penne, roast prime rib, veal saltimbocca, or seared venison. *Dinner only. 6101 Midnight Pass Rd., 941-349-1100. $$-$$$.*

BELLA ROMA

Improbably placed on the upstairs level of a small strip mall, this cozy and delightful Italian restaurant is an intimate spot to share an evening meal. The booths along the window are perhaps the most romantic. Count on classically-prepared Italian cuisine: eggplant rollatine, fried mozzarella, or roasted red peppers for appetizers; homemade stracciatella and minestrone soups; and for the main course, traditional lasagna, ravioli stuffed with spinach and ricotta, veal marsala, veal saltimbocca, grilled salmon with gorgonzola sauce, or the risotta with porcini mushrooms prepared for two. *Dinner only. 5239 Ocean Blvd., 941-349-0995. $$.*

119

PLACES TO DANCE
TREETOP LOUNGE AT THE SUMMERHOUSE
Stairs sweep up to the comfortable bar, cozy tables, and tiny dance floor. A combo plays nightly. *6101 Midnight Pass Rd., 941-349-1100.*

ROMANTIC THINGS TO DO HERE
Watch for dolphins or pelicans diving from the resort's little docks.

Canoe or row to the secluded beach that's just five minutes away.

Drive up to little Siesta Village and the little cluster of shops and restaurants. Get an ice cream cone or a bathing suit or even have lunch.

Walk over to the beach at sunset time and watch for the green flash.

Have a private massage for two outside by your hot tub.

For a kick, stop by Bob's Boathouse *(1310 Old Stickney Point Rd., 941-312-9111).* On your way to the tiki bar, check out the various characters "working" on the dry-docked boats.

Walk through the very aromatic Organic Herb Garden at the Summerhouse *(6101 Midnight Pass Rd., 941-349-1100).*

Rent a little boat and drift for hours. The waterway here has lots of places to explore and you can spend hours putt-putting around. Call Mr. C. B.'s *(1249 Stickney Point Rd., 941-349-4400).*

When you want a picnic for a boat trip or the beach, head up the road to Anna's Delicatessen *(6535 Midnight Pass Rd., 941-349-4888).* Sandwiches are BIG here, but you can get them by the half if you want.

ROMANTIC RADIO
Easy: 88.1FM Jazz: 94.1FM Classical: 90FM
ROMANTIC REMINDERS
What to Bring: Movies for the VCR, wine for midnight stargazing.
Directions: I-75, exit 37. Go west 5 mi. over Stickney Point Bridge to left onto Midnight Pass Rd. Go south 3 mi.

120

ROMANTIC MOVIES

If there's a VCR at your romantic escape bring along some of your favorite tapes. Watching a video together during breakfast, or at midnight, or after a strenuous assortment of activities can be a wonderful, relaxing treat.

And since being in love means laughing and loving and hoping and crying together, the movie choices can be vast. Following is an eclectic gathering of suggestions. Bring some of these or favorites of your own along.

The Bridges of Madison County
Breakfast at Tiffanys
Gone With the Wind
Ghost
Shadowlands
Love Story
Casablanca
Sleepless in Seattle
A Robin Williams tape
You've Got Mail
A Comic Relief tape
One of Peter Seller's Pink Panther series
Message in a Bottle
A Stephen Wright tape
Stir Crazy
A Massage for Lovers tape
A video from Playboy's Making Love Series
An adult selection
Singin' in the Rain
The French Lieutenant's Woman

MORE ROMANTIC IDEAS

☐Spell "I love you" for your love in flower petals.

☐Try stone crab if you are here during the season (October 15 to May 15). It's delicious hot or cold.

☐Buy something. Big, small, inexpensive, or not. Just buy a "memory" of this escape.

☐Fill the tub up with bubbles and settle in. Two people can fit in even the standard-size tubs at the resorts in this book.

☐Have some oysters (cooked not raw) or some green M&Ms. Four oysters are supposed to be the minimum for those remarkable romantic results. No one has yet studied how many green M&Ms it takes.

☐Plan your vacation around the full moon.

☐Plan a trip for your partner but don't say where you are going. Just write a list of what to bring. Or do all the packing yourself.

☐Look for phosphorous at night in the water or even in the seaweed on the beach. Just step on the seaweed and you can see it light up.

☐Give a "trip" gift certificate to your love for a birthday or anniversary. Most lodgings in this book offer them.

CHAPTER 22

A ROMANTIC ESCAPE TO KNIGHT'S ISLAND

AN OVERVIEW

Knight's Island lies off of Florida's southwest coast just west of tiny Cape Haze and north of Fort Myers. It's the setting for very remote Palm Island Resort. When the two of you want to get away from everything, even cars, head to this isolated escape with its two miles of pristine beach and no bridge to the mainland. Cars aren't allowed past the parking lot. You catch a car ferry over and then park for good.

There's not much action here, and what little there is, is of the natural kind. This is a place of laid-back romance, of lazy days and peaceful starlit nights. There's one restaurant and bar but units include full kitchens and if you are coming for more than a weekend, you will want to bring groceries. Families come here because it's a safe place to let kids roam, so there will be children about. But generally you can find your own romantic space, inside or out. The resort is incredibly relaxing, but skip it if your idea of romance includes lots of pampering or fancy restaurant dinners. You're pretty much on your own here and the romantic dinners you have will be the ones you cook yourselves.

LODGING FOR LOVERS
PALM ISLAND RESORT

You won't be pampered at this 200-acre island retreat that looks out at the Gulf of Mexico, but for two people who want to be really alone together and relax, it's a great romantic spot. It's hard to imagine how laid-back this place is until you actually get here and experience it. You can truly spend days here without putting on shoes.

Accommodations are in three-story, pale gray frame buildings with Old Florida-style tin roofs. The one-bedroom apartments facing the water (called Gulf Front Beach Villas) are perfect for a romantic escape. The layout makes great use of 800 square feet and you can live here comfortably. The living-dining area opens onto a balcony perfect for morning coffee or a candlelit dinner. The kitchen is fully equipped.

You won't find a lot of hangers in the closets here because no one who comes here needs many clothes. In the summer months you could easily get by with a bathing suit or two, a cover-up, something with long sleeves for breezy nights or protection from the sun, and a bathrobe for breakfast on the balcony. So pack light. Use the extra luggage space for books, your favorite videos, or if you are into gourmet cooking, unusual culinary items for your romantic dinners.

Maid service is not included but is available daily or twice weekly for a charge. There's a washer/dryer in the unit and extra towels and it's actually quite relaxing to never have someone knock on your door.

Catch the car ferry at the marina on the mainland (check-in is on the island). The ferry makes the run back and forth from 7:00 a.m. until 10:00 p.m. (11:00 p.m. on weekends). A "people-only" boat also operates from noon until evening, for those who want to dine at Leverocks Restaurant at the marina or for those boaters who want to come to the Rum Bay Restaurant for dinner.

4 pools, 11 tennis courts and pro shop, horse shoes, croquet, store. Check-out 11:00 a.m. Romantic Packages. 200 apartments with full kitchens. 7092 Placida Rd., Cape Haze, 33946. Reservations: 800-824-5412. Tel: 941-697-4800. Fax: 941-697-0696. Web: www.palmisland.com. $180-$310.

124

RUM BAY RESTAURANT AND BAR

This is the only restaurant on the island and it's not open for breakfast. Despite the fact that it can be busy and sometimes filled with children, the atmosphere here is still quite pleasant. The food is simple but good and the menu is nicely varied—great baby back ribs, grilled local grouper or shrimp, burgers, pizzas, vegetarian dishes, salads, and pasta. The bar usually features an "island drink" at happy hour. *$-$$.*

ROMANTIC THINGS TO DO HERE

Rent a little power boat and drift through the mangroves. You can also rent canoes, snorkeling equipment, kayaks, windsurfers, and bikes.

Sign up for a turtle walk and learn how they are protected here.

Go fishing. Even if you never have. Bait and fishing tackle can be rented and it's pretty easy to catch a fish in these waters.

Look for falling stars. Pull two beach chairs down to the water's edge, or snuggle together in one chair and just look up at the glorious sky.

See the green flash at sunset or day break from night from the balcony.

If you get island fever, take a cruise to see the sunset or to Useppa Ialand for the day or go to Leverock's on the mainland for dinner.

ROMANTIC RADIO

Easy: 104.9FM

ROMANTIC REMINDERS

What to Bring: Bathrobes (you'll be in them more than anything else), prescription medicine, shampoo or anything you are fussy about (the little convenience store has the basics but not necessarily your brand), sturdy shoes for walking the rockier parts of the shoreline, candles for romantic dinners, your favorite wines or champagnes, laundry soap (dishwasher soap is provided). You can rent VCRs and tapes, but bring your favorites. The on-island store has mostly frozen and canned goods and your best bet is to stop at a supermarket on the way. Do get some special treats. This is a great place to have some romantic meals together.

Directions: I-75, exit 34. Right on River Rd. Cross US41. Continue 7 mi. to traffic light at Pine St. Turn left and go 7 mi. to large ferry sign on right.

125

I will always love you

(following is an anniversary note — written from the heart)

I will always love you

I will never leave you

I will be by your side and stay by your side
as long as we shall live (and beyond)

You are the love of my life
I did not know love like this existed
but I had always hoped

I found true love when I found you

I also found love with you was
even better than I had ever imagined

You are the love of my life, my love

I love you every moment
from the night when you are sleeping by my side
to the morning when you wake up and smile at me
to the evening again when you touch me
or hold me by your side

I miss you when we are apart and
love the things we do together
whether we are playing or working or just being

I love you

CHAPTER 23

A ROMANTIC ESCAPE TO SANIBEL ISLAND

AN OVERVIEW

Sanibel is a barrier island off the coast of Fort Myers in southwest Florida. It's connected to the mainland by a three-mile-long causeway. Both sides of the island are spectacular. Shell-filled beaches face out to the Gulf of Mexico. Across the island are wetlands and marshes and beautiful San Carlos Bay which is sprinkled with hundreds of tiny green puffs of uninhabited islets.

Sanibel Island is far enough south to be almost always warm and is a popular winter destination. There are many resorts and motels here and the one main road that runs the length of the island can be incredibly trafficky in the winter months. For a romantic escape on Sanibel, nothing beats the Song of the Sea. Off the traveled path, it's a small secluded hideaway set back from the beach among palm trees and Australian pines. Comfortable condo-like units have full kitchens but the rest of the property is more like an inn, from the cozy common living room where a scrumptious continental breakfast is served to the caring management to room service from the excellent restaurant that is right next door.

LODGING FOR LOVERS
SONG OF THE SEA

At this charming and secluded beachfront prize, you can really relax. You can live in your bathing suit and cook in your room, walk to an excellent restaurant (which will also deliver), spend your days looking for shells or biking, or order a pizza in and watch a movie on the VCR.

From the moment you arrive here, you know this place is special. The entrance is terrific. You check in at a little desk in a warm welcoming living room and then you drive through an archway and you know you've escaped to a peaceful world.

Rooms are in appealing two-story pink stucco buildings. They aren't romantically decorated but they are exceptionally comfortable and easy to relax in. If you want some space and an unbeatable view, go for the beachfront one-bedroom suites. There's a dark and cozy bedroom that you can sleep in all day. A full kitchen runs along the hallway to the dining and living area. Sliding glass doors lead to a large, private balcony. The view is picture-perfect: green grass, sand dunes, striped beach umbrellas in a row, and the turquoise Gulf beyond.

The grounds are grassy and there's an outdoor grill (if you feel like cooking) and a nice-size pool. The beach is full of shells and you can clean off your finds of the day in the little "shelling" hut.

Everything is easy here. For breakfast delicious rolls, breads, fruits, and pastries are laid out. Toss a coin and see which one of you brings it back on the thoughtfully provided trays. For dinner the two of you can walk next door to Portofino, an excellent Italian restaurant. Or dial 316 and they'll deliver right to your room. It's incredibly peaceful and quiet here. This is one of the South Seas Resorts and you can use your Song of the Sea charge card at their other Sanibel resorts. A complimentary trolley runs between them Monday through Saturday.

Pool, whirlpool, grill, bicycles, shuffleboard. Children welcome. Check-out 11:00 a.m. Romantic Packages. 30 units. General Manager: Linda Logan. 863 East Gulf Dr., Sanibel Island, 33957. Reservations: 800-231-1045. Tel: 941-472-2220. Fax: 941-481-4947. Web: www.southseas.com. $160-$420.

RESTAURANTS FOR LOVERS

PORTOFINO

Next door to the Song of the Sea is this intimate and romantic northern Italian restaurant. A pianist plays gentle background music weekends. Low walls and groupings of plants create numerous discrete dining areas. Do listen to the daily specials. If you want anything not on the menu, just ask. Sharing the antipasto for two is a perfect way to begin the meal together here. The minestrone or any of the salads are also good choices. For an entree, try the veal saltimbocca or veal marsala or any of the pasta dishes. The rich bolognese sauce comes with fettucini but it's also excellent over spaghetti. If you want them to deliver to your room, just call. *937 East Gulf Dr., 941-472-0494. $$.*

WINDOWS ON THE WATER

This restaurant is in a resort and you have to walk through a sometimes hectic reception area to get here, but once you step inside you'll find a quiet, intimate atmosphere. Tables are on two levels and diners have a terrific view of the Gulf through floor-to-ceiling windows. Dine on surf and turf, local grouper, seafood pad Thai, or their signature dish, tender "Duck Noopie." *Sundial Beach Resort, 1451 Middle Gulf Dr., 941-395-6014. $$.*

THISTLE LODGE

This appealing restaurant overlooks the Gulf of Mexico and is designed to resemble a Victorian-style house, but with floor-to-ceiling windows that show off the view. Tables are in several small rooms and arranged so that most have great water views. Entrees include Florida lobster thermador, a spicy seafood paella, Jamaican jerk pork, and grilled N.Y. strip with a rum-barbeque sauce. Upstairs is a bar and lounge with even better water views. *Casa Ybel Resort, 2255 West Gulf Dr., 941-472-9200. $$.*

ROMANTIC THINGS TO DO IN SANIBEL

Get married or renew your vows barefoot on the beach at sunset or even romantically drifting along in a boat. Call Patricia Slater at Weddings by the Sea (*941-472-8712*). Sometimes she only needs a few hours advance notice, so you can almost do this on the spur of the moment!

Go to a spa together. Try a relaxing aromatherapy massage or a honeysuckle scrub or a warm herbal wrap or splurge and get a his-and-hers Royal Spoil—a full day of gentle pampering or create your very own package. Call Day Spa of Sanibel (*2075 Periwinkle Way at Periwinkle Place, 941-395-2220*) for a complete list of services.

Stop in the 32 little shops at Periwinkle Place. The Brown Bag (*941-472-1171*) carries casual clothes for men. The Beach House (*941-472-2676*) has an enormous selection of swimsuits, including Gottex and Elizabeth Stewart. At Island Style (*941-472-4343*) you'll find one-of-a-kind pieces of jewelry, pottery, and sculpture.

Buy each other a surprise gift. You'll find pendants, bracelets, necklaces, and earrings made of 14K gold and fashioned into shells, sand dollars, or exquisitely delicate dolphins at Sanibel Goldsmith (*2055 Periwinkle Way, 941-472-8677*).

For an incredibly romantic moonlit evening on the water, call Wildside Adventures (*15041 Captiva Drive at McCarthy's Marina, 941-395-2925*). They'll lead just the two of you (in your own two-person kayak) out to the middle of calm Pine Island Sound on a starlit or moonlit night. You can also rent a two-person kayak or a canoe and paddle around by yourselves during the day.

Check out the J.N. "Ding" Darling National Wildlife Preserve. It covers half of the island and is home to numerous birds, turtles, marsh hares, bobcats, and alligators. Bike or drive the five-mile Wildlife Drive or hike the trails or go canoeing. If you want to spot great birds, come just after dawn or just before dusk.

ROMANTIC RADIO
Easy: 104.1FM   Country: 92.9FM Oldies: 100FM
ROMANTIC REMINDERS
What to Bring: Your favorite VCR tapes, fun ingredients if you plan to cook, perhaps a nice bottle of bubbly for a late night stroll on the beach.
Directions: I-75, exit 21. Take Daniels Road West. Cross US 41 and continue to the Sanibel Causeway. Call Sanibel-Captiva Airport Shuttle (800-395-9524 or locally 466-3236) if you want to be picked up at the airport. They'll even go to Miami or Fort Lauderdale, which may be your quickest air connection.

LOVELY THOUGHTS

"I'm back to livin' Floridays, blue skys and
ultra violet rays, lookin' for better days."
- Jimmy Buffett

"I was a child and she was a child,
In this kingdom by the sea;
But we loved with a love that was more than
love -
I and my Annabel Lee."
- Edgar Allan Poe

"A joy that is shared
is a joy made double."
- English Proverb

"The grand essentials of happiness are:
something to do, someone to love,
and something to hope for."
- Allan Chalmers

"I took the good times,
I'll take the bad times,
I'll take you just the way you are."
- Billy Joel

"Follow your bliss."
- Joseph Campbell

WHO'S IN CHARGE HERE, ANYWAY?

You two are. You're going on a special romantic retreat and you're paying for it. You're in charge. From choosing your special journey to returning home to a special evening, the two of you are in control.

The first way to take control is be sure you choose the "escape" that you really want. They're all great in their own way. Make sure their way matches yours.

If you have any questions, call the property. These properties are here partially because they do special things for people in love. They'll answer any questions and help you with choices.

If a property has a special "romance package" don't be afraid to ask them to "personalize" it for the two of you. If they offer a welcome bottle of champagne and you'd rather have a chardonnay or orange juice, ask!

The properties in this book respond well to requests. So do many of the restaurants. That's one of the reasons they were included here.

For example, if you want to "sleep in" all day put out a no-disturb sign and tell the desk/innkeeper you want absolutely no calls except emergencies. If you want something not on the menu, ask. If you want softer or more pillows, just ask. From flowers to flute music, balloons to bagels, whatever you want to have or have happen, just ask.

CHAPTER 24

A ROMANTIC ESCAPE TO NORTH NAPLES

AN OVERVIEW

A small section of southwest Florida is not bordered by barrier islands and the western edge of the mainland is one long stunning stretch of beach that looks right out to the Gulf of Mexico. At the south end of this strip is the affluent and sophisticated town of Naples. In the last few years there has been tremendous development just to the north of downtown, and what was once extremely rural is now an exclusive neighborhood known as North Naples, with its own set of fine restaurants and fancy shops.

North Naples has many lodging choices, but for a truly romantic escape, nothing beats the Registry Resort. When the two of you want to stay in a classy, full-service hotel that you won't want to leave, with a great restaurant, an elegant bar, a disco, one of the best Sunday brunches anywhere, a nature preserve, a beach on the Gulf of Mexico, and a spa for massages and herbal wraps, but you also want the choice of many sophisticated restaurants and even the symphony practically out your front door, this is the place to come.

LODGING FOR LOVERS
NAPLES REGISTRY RESORT

It's the resort itself and the experience of being here that makes it so romantic. The service is superb and if it rained for your entire stay you could still have a wonderfully romantic time.

The Registry is an 18-story high-rise that looks out over the mangroves of Clam Pass Sanctuary and beyond to the Gulf of Mexico. Guest rooms are painted in deep shades of pink or green and heavy draperies keep out the light when you want to sleep. This is a room you can stay in all day, sending down for meals, curled up in thick terry Registry bathrobes watching movies and snoozing. From your balcony you can scan the twinkling night sky or watch the sun slip into the Gulf.

The resort is truly self-contained. In the lobby is an elegant bar (afternoon tea is served here), a great gift shop, the award-winning Lafite restaurant, and Cafe Chablis and its fabulous Sunday brunch. On a boardwalk just outside the lobby is an ice cream and patisserie shop, several terrific little boutiques, an art gallery, the Brass Pelican restaurant for steak and seafood, and the Club Zanzibar disco.

There's a terrific spa with exercise equipment that faces the view. Come here together for a his-and-hers algae full body mask or get yourselves wrapped in sea mud or have therapeutic massages together in the privacy of your room.

When the two of you feel like enjoying the outdoor possibilities, there's plenty to do without leaving the resort. Go for a swim or sit by the pool. Take a tram ride or walk along the half-mile boardwalk to the beach. Learn to sail a Hobie Cat or rent a canoe or a kayak and explore the quiet waters of Clam Pass Sanctuary. Take a tennis lesson for two or get a bicycle for two (rent them at the Towel Stand) and pedal around the quiet residential streets of Pelican Bay.

Pool, spa, 15 tennis courts and pro shop. Many non-smoking floors. Check-out 12 noon. Romantic Packages. 474 rooms. 475 Seagate Dr., Naples, 33940. Reservations: 800-247-9810. Tel: 941-597-3232. Fax: 941-597-3232. Web: www.registrieshotels.com. $230-$450.

A RESTAURANT FOR LOVERS
LAFITE

When you are in the mood for an elegant and romantic dinner step into the celebrated Lafite, with walls of rich, dark wood and dim light softly glowing from the candles on the tables and the ceiling chandeliers. There are several intimate dining rooms and the atmosphere is quiet and formal. The innovative, globally-inspired menu changes yearly but includes such creations as pine nut crusted goat cheese, Hudson Valley fois gras, tuna with Japanese horseradish, Moroccan rack of lamb, and pan-seared tiger prawns. The wine list is extensive. *Days closed vary. Reservations essential. 941-597-3232, ext. 5666. $$$.*

THE REGISTRY'S DISCO
CLUB ZANZIBAR

Naples hottest nightclub is right at the Registry, just across from the lobby entrance and this multi-level "happening-place" is packed on weekends—strobe lights, dry ice "smoke" tumbling down on the crush of dancers, everyone immersed in the latest dance craze. The second floor balcony is packed with on-lookers. If discos fit into your idea of romance, you'll love it here. If the two of you used to like these places, but think you're "too old" now, well, go on in anyway and check it out. You only live once. During the week it's a lot quieter and there's a much better chance of catching a slow song. *9:00 p.m.-2:00 a.m. Closed Mon., 941-597-3232, ext. 5645.*

A GREAT ROMANTIC BRUNCH
CAFE CHABLIS

This refined and elegant brunch is one of the best-tasting and most beautifully-presented brunches ever. You'll need to dress up a bit; it's a social event. The menu looks impressive but it doesn't even begin to cover the choices—made-to-order omelettes, waffles, several roasts, platters and platters of perfectly arranged fresh and grilled vegetables, pates, cheeses, iced shrimp, smoked oysters, chafing dishes of eggs Benedict, chicken and veal dishes, cakes and pies and cookies. Do start with a small sampling (you'll keep discovering new items you want to try) and don't check out on a Sunday if you like brunches. You'll want a long and leisurely nap after this one. *941-597-3232, ext. 5828.*

A NEARBY RESTAURANT FOR LOVERS
VILLA PESCATORE
Naples has numerous great restaurants. Check with the Registry's concierge for recommendations and menus. For a quiet and romantic evening near the Registry, try the Villa Pescatore. It's about five minutes by car. A pianist entertains most evenings in the cozy bar at this dark, romantic Italian spot. Dinner is served in several rooms at well-spaced tables. The spinach salad with walnuts and the fresh mozzarella with basil and tomatoes make excellent first choices. Veal, filet mignon, free-range chicken, and a choice of pasta dishes are just some of the entrees. If you don't see what you want, ask. Lovers of Italian wines will enjoy the wine list, which includes a great selection of Tuscan reds. *8920 Tamiami Trail North. 941-597-8119. $$.*

ROMANTIC THINGS TO DO HERE
On a calm day, rent a small boat and spend the morning offshore. Parkshore Marina *(4310 Gulf Shore Blvd. N., 941-434-0724)* rents 20' powerboats and 25' pontoon boats. A half-day for two people costs between $119 and $129.

Catch great jazz at the Backstage Tap & Grill *(Waterside Shops, 941-598-1300)* Wednesday and Saturday and guitar Thursday and Friday.

Browse through the upscale offerings at the nearby Waterside Shops at Pelican Bay where you'll find Saks Fifth Avenue, Ann Taylor, Banana Republic, Williams-Sonoma, and much more among waterfalls and wooden walkways. Stop in for pizza at California Pizza Kitchen.

Paddle a canoe together through the Registry's backyard. You may see blue herons, brown pelicans, roseate spoonbills, cormorants, osprey, loggerhead turtles, horseshoe crabs, and river otters.

ROMANTIC RADIO
Easy: 105.1FM   Jazz: 98.9FM   Country: 107FM
ROMANTIC REMINDERS
What to Bring: Smart resortwear plus something dressy for Lafite.
Directions: I-75, exit 16. Go west on Pine Ridge Rd. (Rt. 896), across Rt. 41 (Pine Ridge Rd. becomes Seagate Dr.) to entrance.

HELPFUL INFORMATION

LODGING RATES

The ranges given in this book are for two people and do not include taxes or gratuities.

The lower number is generally the lowest off-season rate and/or the smallest room. The higher number is generally the highest on-season rate and/or the nicest room or suite.

Bear in mind that these are the published rates of the properties. Off-season it is well worth inquiring if there is a lower rate available or a special, off-season package. Sometimes a package will include a meal or two plus a room and the total will be less than the rate for just the room alone.

In fact, all year round it is worth asking, when you are making your reservations, if there are special packages or rates available.

All properties in this book have at least one handicapped-accessible room except the Plantation-Manor Inn, Harborfront Inn, and Palm Island Resort.

RESTAURANT RATES

Rates are for two people, without beverages. When a range is given, the high end is based on having all courses and choosing the highest-priced items.

$= up to $30
$$=$30-$60
$$$= $60-up

CAR RENTAL NUMBERS

Alamo 800-327-9633
Avis 800-331-1212
Budget 800-527-0700
Hertz 800-654-3131
National 800-227-7368
Thrifty 800-367-2277

AIRLINE NUMBERS

American 800-433-7300
Continental 800-523-3273
Delta 800-221-2121
Northwest 800-225-2525
TWA 800-221-2000
U.S. Air 800-428-4322

Amelia Island Chamber of Commerce
102 Centre Street
Fernandina Beach, FL 32035
800-226-3542

Anna Maria Island Chamber of Commerce
501 W. Manatee Avenue
Holmes Beach, FL 34217
813-778-1541

Daytona Beach Chamber of Commerce
126 E. Orange Ave.
Daytona Beach, FL 32114
904-255-0981

Delray Beach Chamber of Commerce
64 S.E. 5th Avenue
Delray Beach, FL 33483
561-278-0424

Fort Lauderdale Chamber of Commerce
512 N.E. 3rd Avenue
Fort Lauderdale, FL 33301
954-462-6000

Jacksonville Chamber of Commerce
3 Independence Drive
Jacksonville, FL 32202
800-733-2668

Lake Wales Chamber of Commerce
340 W. Central Avenue
Lake Wales, FL 33859
941-676-3445

Mount Dora Chamber of Commerce
341 Alexander Street
Mount Dora, FL 32757
352-383-2165

Naples Visitors Center
1074 5th Avenue South
Naples, FL 33940
941-643-1919

New Smyrna Beach Chamber of Commerce
115 Canal Street
New Smyrna Beach, FL 32168
800-541-9621

Orlando Chamber of Commerce
75 E. Ivanhoe Boulevard
Orlando, FL 32804
407-425-1234

Palm Beach Chamber of Commerce
45 Cocoanut Row
Palm Beach, FL 33480
561-655-3282

Palm Island/Charlotte County Chamber of Commerce
2702 Tamiami Trail
Port Charlotte, FL 33950
941-627-2222

Sanibel Visitors Center
1159 Causeway Road
Sanibel, FL 33957
941-472-1080

Sarasota Visitor Information Center
6555 N. Tamiami Trail
Sarasota, FL 34236
800-522-9799

Seaside Chamber of Commerce
County Road 30-A (Box 4730)
Santa Rosa Beach, FL 32459
904-231-4224

St. Augustine/St. John's County Visitors Bureau
1 Riberia St.
St. Augustine, FL 32084
904-829-5681

Stuart Chamber of Commerce
1650 S.W. Kanner Highway
Stuart, FL 34994
561-287-1088

Tallahassee Visitors Bureau
South Duval Street
Tallahassee, FL 32302
800-628-2866

Winter Park Chamber of Commerce
150 N. New York Avenue
Winter Park, FL 32789
407-644-8281

INDEX

ABOUT THE AUTHORS

Pamela Acheson and Dick Myers are husband and wife. Since their escape from corporate New York over a decade ago, they have explored, lived in, and written about romantic Florida and the Caribbean.

They both contribute to numerous national and international magazines and between them they have authored over a dozen books including *The Best Romantic Escapes in Florida, More of the Best Romantic Escapes in Florida, The Best of the British Virgin Islands, Visiting the Virgin Islands with the Kids*, and *The Best of St. Thomas and St. John, U.S. Virgin Islands*.

In addition Ms. Acheson also writes for several editions of Fodor's Travel Guides including Fodor's Florida, Fodor's Caribbean, Fodor's Virgin Islands, and Fodor's Ports of Call. And Mr. Myers is the author of the acclaimed instructional book *Tennis for Humans: A Simple Blueprint for Winning*.

When they are not traveling and exploring, Pam and Dick divide their time between the British Virgin Islands and the Sunshine State.

More great reviews for
The Best Romantic Escapes in Florida
series
(continued from page one)

"Pick up this book! It has a lot of great ideas"
—News Center 6, Orlando

"This is a great book."
— NBC News 2 Midday

"A lighthearted guidebook...full of insider tips and recommendations."
—Essentially America

"Pamela Acheson and Dick Myers are the quintessential experts on romantic Florida."
—Hugh Benjamin
author, A Place Like This

"Romantic choices for everyone, from small inns and quaint hotels to barefoot beach escapes and sophisticated seaside resorts."
—The Midwest Book Review

"The focus is on romance, with tried and tested hints and off-the-beaten-path destinations."
—The New Smyrna Beach Observer

"Lush locales and exquisite eateries...also tips on how to best prepare for a romantic trip to paradise."
—Ft. Lauderdale Sun-Sentinel